Kwezuonu!
A Beginner's Guide to the Igbo Language

Chinemerem Nwanze

featuring foreword by Okey Ndibe
Cover by Ekeocha Nnaemeka

Copyright © 2019 by Chinemerem Nwanze.

All rights reserved, including the right to reproduce this book or portions thereof in any form whatsoever. For more information address YBF Publishing LLC
PO Box 361526 Decatur, GA 30036

ISBN#: 978-1-950279-04-3
LOC Number: 2019901065

Edited + Formatted by The Literary Revolutionary + Team

Manufactured in the United States of America

For information regarding special discounts for bulk purchases, please contact The Literary Revolutionary Special Sales Team at 470-396-0660 or support@theliteraryrevolutionary.com

**Follow Chinemerem!
Instagram: @Chinemrm**

Kwezuonu!
A Beginner's Guide to the Igbo Language

Please complete the following sections:

This Book Belongs To:

_____

My Reason for Wanting to Learn Igbo:

_____
_____
_____
_____

Goals for Igbo Learning Journey:

_____
_____
_____
_____

Table of Contents

Foreword - Okey Ndibe 7
Introduction 11

Part 1: Igbo Alphabet and Vocabulary 15
Chapter 1 - What is Igbo? 17
Chapter 2 - The Igbo Alphabet 23
Chapter 3 - Igbo Vocabulary + Parts of Speech 35

Part 2: Fundamentals of Igbo Grammar 69
Chapter 4 - Tone Marks 71
Chapter 5 - Igbo Pronouns 75
Cumulative Skills Test (Chapters 1 - 5) 88
Chapter 6 - Verbs, Tenses, Commands, and Negations 93
Chapter 7 - Additional Practice 127

Part 3 - Culture and Resources 135
Chapter 8 - Igbo Learning Resources 137
Chapter 9 - List of Igbo Names 143
Chapter 10 - Skills Test Answers 153
Acknowledgements 161

DEDICATION
To Ifeanyi, Onyeka, and Izunna

FOREWORD

The first time I spoke to Chinemerem Nwanze, I became a fan. Three things deeply impressed me about her. The first was the pride she took in her ability to speak Igbo language. Even though she has grown up in the US, she is so versed in Igbo that she and I were able to converse in the language. Anybody who pays attention to the state of Igbo language proficiency knows that the vast majority of children born to Igbo parents in the US are bereft of proficiency in Igbo. For that matter, there are also many Igbo youngsters born and raised in Nigeria who are baffled by the language that ought to be their first.

The second reason I admired Chinemerem was her sense of gratitude to her parents for giving her the gift of a mother tongue. It was clear, as she and I spoke, that she recognized the extraordinariness of that gift. She waxed with praise for her parents for taking the time to coach her siblings and her in Igbo.

The third factor has to do with this short book, a labor of love and act of generosity. Troubled that too many of her peers lack the bequest of a language that ought to be part and parcel of their cultural kit, Chinemerem chose to do something about it.

That something is this small gem of a book. It is Chinemerem's summons to her fellow Igbo-descended young women and men to be more receptive to their cultural heritage. It is also the young author's challenge—rebuke is too strong a word, or I would have used it—it is her challenge to Igbo adults, especially parents. Her message to all of us is rather clear: invest the time to teach your children the language and ways of your people.

Much has been made of the Igbo's adventurousness and enterprise. Indeed, the Igbo are dispersed in most parts of the world—and often thrive, thanks to their acumen for industry, adaptability, and innovativeness. Yet, all too often, the Igbo sacrifice their language as the price for success in their new environments.

I suggest—and Chinemerem would agree—that this is too high a price to pay. Language is not just a tool for communication. Language is that, but it also embodies a people's cultural worldview. When a young person is unable to speak her parents' natal language, it means that a cultural and conceptual gulf exists between parent and child. It is a situation that can only impoverish, not vitalize, our children and their relationships with us.

Even though Chinemerem's book is addressed to youngsters, Igbo adults would do well to heed her message. We all need to be better informed about our inner lives, the values that shape our lives, and the language that makes our world come alive in all its splendor and variety.

I expect even greater things from Chinemerem, a driven, purposeful, and visionary girl.

Okey Ndibe | *Author of two novels and a memoir, Never Look an American in the Eye*

INTRODUCTION

Growing up, my parents made it their mission to ensure that I would be immersed in my Nigerian heritage. They started this mission on the day I was born - naming me Chinemerem Ifeoma Nwanze, refusing to give me (and later my siblings) any English names because they wanted us to know that Igbo names were equally as beautiful and meaningful. Although I am immensely appreciative of my parents for this now, I remember feeling so annoyed as a child when my teachers/friends couldn't pronounce my name and insisted on shortening it or giving me weird nicknames. My parents knew that my name would be a major part of my identity - therefore, if my name was fully Igbo, I would have to learn to embrace it and be proud of it.

Then, my parents made a decision that I will never be able to repay them for; **they decided to teach me the Igbo language.**

When my parents made the choice to teach me and my siblings how to speak Igbo, they didn't have much support. Their friends thought they were attempting the impossible, that they were crazy if they thought they could do something so drastic. *"Why are you doing this? You'll confuse them. They won't speak English well,"* were among the things their friends and acquaintances were saying. Nevertheless, my parents persisted. My dad took it upon himself to teach us how to write Igbo, drawing pictures when he taught us the alphabet and bringing back Igbo books whenever he went to Nigeria. At the age of 10, I began lecturing at St. Eugene's Igbo Catholic Church in Los Angeles, and this greatly aided me in expanding my Igbo vocabulary and cultivating my passion for the Igbo culture.

However, I've realized over the years that Igbo isn't being passed down in my generation or even in the generation before mine. I have listened as my friends express frustration at their parents for not teaching them the language and their struggle to feel fully connected to their Igbo culture. I wrote this book because (although it is hard to admit), the Igbo language is dying and will soon become extinct unless something is done. It is our job to keep it alive and to continue to pass it down.

The Igbo people have a very popular chant that they use to greet, identify and unite: *"Cha cha cha Igbo Kwenu! Ya! Cha cha cha Igbo Kwenu! Ya! Igbo Kwezuonu!"*

I decided to title this book **Kwezuonu!** because the Igbo language is something we should be proud of, something we should claim, and something that should unify us regardless of where we are from. *Kwezuonu* is a collective agreement. With one mind, we can work towards keeping the Igbo language alive.

To whoever is reading this, I hope this book aids you in your journey to learning how to speak the Igbo language. It won't be easy, but I'm proud of you for being willing to keep this language alive for generations to come. Your determination will lead to great results and together we will make sure that Igbo never dies. ***Igbo Kwenu!***

PART ONE
Igbo Alphabet + Vocabulary

Chapter One
WHAT IS IGBO?

Important Note: The word "Igbo" can be used to refer to Igbo language, Igbo land, and Igbo people.

IGBO LANGUAGE

The Igbo language, commonly referred to as *asụsụ Igbo*, is one of Nigeria's official languages and the native language of one of Nigeria's three major tribes, the Igbo people. Among the Benue - Congo sub branch of the Niger - Congo** family of languages, Igbo is a tonal language. Roughly 20 million people worldwide speak the Igbo language, a majority of speakers residing in southeastern Nigeria[1]. However, Igbo is also spoken and recognized as a minority language in Equatorial Guinea.

The Igbo language has many different dialects, which include Onitsha, Ikwerre, Anambra, Orlu, and Owerri. In fact, different geographical areas of Igboland have distinct variations of the varying dialects, which

---

[1] Igboanusi, Herbert (2006). *Agents of Progress or Problem-Makers?: Missionary Activities in the Development of the Igbo Language.* Accessed through:
https://www.researchgate.net/publication/32171087_AGENTS_OF_PROGRESS_OR_PROBLEM-MAKERS_MISSIONARY_ACTIVITIES_IN_THE_DEVELOPMENT_OF_THE_IGBO_LANGUAGE

can be easily identified. Though there are variations in words and pronunciation in each dialect, it typically doesn't stop Igbo speakers from understanding each other. When it comes to written Igbo, central Igbo is typically used since it is standardized. Set by Dr. S.E. Onwu and an eleven-man committee in 1961, central Igbo is essentially a mixture of varying dialects.[2]

What is a Niger - Congo Language?

Niger - Congo languages are a group of languages that constitute one of the world's largest language families and are spoken primarily throughout Sub-Saharan Africa. These languages are split into nine subfamilies: Benue - Congo, Kwa, Atlantic, Mande, Ijoid, Kordofanian, Kru, Gur, and Adamawa-Ubangi. **Igbo falls under the Benue - Congo sub family, which is the most substantial. Like Igbo, a majority of Niger - Congo languages are tonal, meaning that they use pitch to distinguish between words with the same spelling.**

Other examples of Niger - Congo languages include: Yoruba, Lingala, Wolof, Swahili and Shona.

---

[2] Pritchett, Frances W. (n.d.). *A History of the Igbo Language.* Accessed through:
http://www.columbia.edu/itc/mealac/pritchett/00fwp/igbo/igbohistory.html

IGBO LAND

Igboland is located in southeastern Nigeria and consists of 7 states, 5 of which are predominantly Igbo:
- Abia State
- Anambra State
- Enugu State
- Ebonyi State
- Imo State
- *Delta State**
- *Rivers State**

Igboland is divided in two by the River Niger, and the division in unequal. The bigger half is located on the east of the River Niger and includes Abia, Enugu, Imo, Anambra, and the Igbo speaking parts of Rivers State (Ahoada, Elele, Etche, Obibo, and more). The smaller half includes Igbo speaking areas of Delta State such as Asaba, Ogwashi Ukwu, Kwale, Igbuzo, and more[3].

Delta and Rivers State are part of Igboland and some Igbo people reside in these areas and speak the Igbo language. These states are not majority Igbo, seeing as the Igbo population in these areas is roughly 25%[4].

---

[3] Ihejirika, Okechukwu C. (1997). *Igbo For Learners 1*. Ibadan: Onibonoje Press
[4] UC Riverside Faculty (n.d.) *The Igbo of Nigeria: History and Culture*. Accessed through: http://www.faculty.ucr.edu/~legneref/igbo/igbo2.htm

IGBO PEOPLE IN POPULAR CULTURE

Igbo people have been making an impact all over the world in a plethora of ways. Here is a list of notable Igbo people in popular culture:

- **Chinua Achebe** *(1930 - 2013) - Author*
- **Chimamanda Adichie** *(1977 - present) - Author*
- **Christopher Okigbo** *(1932 - 1967) - Poet*
- **Buchi Emecheta** *(1944 - 2017) - Author*
- **Chiwetel Ejiofor** *(1977 - present) - Actor*
- **Patience Ozokwor** *(1958 - present) - Actress*
- **Nnamdi Azikiwe** *(1904 - 1996) - Politician, first president of the Republic of Nigeria*
- **Chukwuemeka Odumegwu Ojukwu** *(1933 - 2011) - Former Biafran Head of State*
- **Cardinal Francis Arinze** *(1932 - present) - First native African archbishop of the Catholic Church diocese in Onitsha, Nigeria*
- **Jidenna Mobisson** *(1985 - present) - Musician, Songwriter*
- **Ken Nwadiogbu** *(1994 - present) - Visual artist*
- **Chief Stephen Osita Osadebe** *(1936 - 2007) - Musician*
- **Ugo Mozie** *(1991 - present) - Creative executive*
- **Ngozi Iweala** *(1954 - present) - Economist*
- **Festus Ezeli** *(1989 - present) - Basketball player*
- **Alex Iwobi** *(1996 - present) - Soccer player*

- *Jay Jay Okocha (1973 - present) - Soccer player*
- *Emma Nyra (1988 - present) - Musician*
- *Amaka Igwe (1963 - 2014) - Filmmaker*
- *Pius Okigbo (1924 - 2000) - Economist*

Artist Ken Nwadiogbu at work[5]

---
[5] Photo courtesy of Ken Nwadiogbu - Instagram: @kennwadiogbu

Chapter Two
Unit One
THE IGBO ALPHABET

The Igbo Alphabet, *also known as Abịdịị,* has **36 letters**. The alphabet in this book is centralized and is the most commonly used, but you may see additional consonants in different dialects.

To make this easier, I'm going to write the alphabet using English words that sound like the pronunciation of each letter. However, some letters do not have English sound equivalents - so I will use Igbo words for these particular letters.

THE IGBO ALPHABET

A - sound: apple
B - sound: beat
Ch - sound: Charlie
D - sound: deep
E - sound: egg
F - sound: fish
G - sound: gear
GB - sound: Igbo
GH - sound: ighe
GW - sound: Gwendolyn
H - sound: house
I - sound: eat

Ị - sound: internet
J - sound: jam
K - sound: kind
KP - sound: Akpịrị
KW - sound: quite
L - sound: like
M - sound: made
N - sound: news
Ṅ - sound: song
NW - sound: want
NY - sound: venue
O - sound: orange
Ọ - sound: auto

P - sound: pop
R - sound: reduce
S - sound: sell
SH - sound: share
T - sound: tea
U - sound: spoon

Ụ - sound: spurn
V - sound: value
W - sound: way
Y - sound: yellow
Z - sound: zero

VOWELS IN THE IGBO ALPHABET (ỤDAUME)

Vowels are sounds that are produced from the vibration of our vocal cords, without blocking air flow into our mouths. In English, the vowels are:

A   E   I   O   U

The Igbo alphabet has 8 vowels, also known as *ụdaume*. The *ụdaume* might resemble the English vowels, but there are dotted vowels (Ị, Ọ, Ụ) included. The Igbo vowels are:

A   E   I   Ị   O   Ọ   U   Ụ

Of the eight vowels, there are dots under three of them. While this might seem insignificant, these dots under the I, O, and U make them sound different - longer - than the I, O, and U without dots.

All Igbo vowels with the exception of U and Ụ can be used as individual words.

Example: **Ọ na eri nri. (She / He / It / is eating).** In this example, "**Ọ**" is used as a pronoun.

CONSONANTS IN THE IGBO LANGUAGE

Consonants are sounds that we make as a result of some blocking of air flow into our mouths. In the Igbo alphabet, there are 28 consonants total. Of the 28 consonants, there are 9 double consonants, which are:

CH   GB   GH   GW   KP   KW   NW
NY   SH

Keep in Mind: Even though these double consonants have 2 letters, they are each still considered one letter of the Igbo alphabet.

SPECIAL LETTERS

There are 2 letters in the Igbo alphabet that are neither vowels or consonants. Sometimes, these letters can be used as vowels. However, they can also show up as consonants. As a result, they are usually referred to as semivowels, but are included in the consonant count. These letters are:

                M   N

Examples of M and N as a semi - vowels:

Mma (knife)   Nna (father)
Mgbe (when)   Nne (mother)
Mbe (turtle)   Nri (food)

CHAPTER 2 UNIT 1 - SKILLS TEST

1. How many letters are in the *standard* Igbo Alphabet?
   a. 26
   b. 40
   c. 36
   d. 19

2. How many Igbo letters are in **Nwanze**?
   a. 5
   b. 7
   c. 4
   d. 6

3. How many Igbo letters are in **aka**?
   a. 9
   b. 3
   c. 10
   d. 4

4. What is another name for the Igbo alphabet?
   a. Abc
   b. Letters
   c. Abịdịị
   d. Abcde

5. What are vowels called in Igbo?

6. How many consonants are in the Igbo language? How many double consonants?

7. Which of the following are semi vowels? Circle all that apply.
    a. M
    b. B
    c. GB
    d. N
    e. F
    f. KW

8. Can you say the Igbo alphabet without looking at the list on top?

Chapter Two
Unit Two

VOWEL HARMONY

In the Igbo sound system, vowel harmony is the pairing of vowels from the same vowel group - and there are two vowel groups in the Igbo language. Each vowel group contains four letters.

THE "A" GROUP
The first Igbo vowel group is called the **A group**. It is sometimes referred to as the dotted vowel group since three of the vowels have dots under them. The vowels in the **A group** are:

A Ị Ọ Ụ

A group vowels are usually paired with one another - meaning that any **Igbo words containing the vowel "a"** will be **paired with** *another a* or *the dotted i, o or u.*

Examples:
- akwụkwọ (book) - This shows a combination of the **a**, dotted **u**, and dotted **o**.
- achịcha (bread) - This shows a combination of the **a** and the dotted **i**.

- aka (hand) - This shows a combination of the **a** and another **a**.

Even if a word doesn't contain the letter "a", the dotted vowels in the **A group** still need to be paired together. For example:
- ụlọ (house) - This is a pairing between the dotted **u** and dotted **o**.
- ụkwụ (foot) - This is a pairing between a dotted **u** and another dotted **u**.

Note: *A group vowels are considered the "light vowel" group, because the vocal cords do not vibrate when these vowels are pronounced.*

THE "E" GROUP
The second Igbo vowel group is called the *E group*. It is sometimes called the undotted group because none of the vowels in this group are dotted. The vowels in the E group are:

E   I   O   U

Like the A group vowels, E group vowels must be paired with one another - only this time, **words containing the vowel "e" will be paired with** *another e or an undotted i, o, or u.*

Examples:
- eze (teeth / king) - This is a combination of the **e** and another **e**.

- ire (tongue) - This is a combination of the undotted **i** and the **e**.
- oche (chair) - This is a combination of the undotted **o** and the **e**.
- ube (pear / spear) - This is a combination of the undotted **u** and the **e**.

Even if a word doesn't contain the letter "e", the undotted vowels with the **exception of "a"** should still be paired together.

Examples:
- iko (cup) - This is a pairing between the undotted **o** and the undotted **i**.
- ukwu (waist) - This is a pairing between the undotted **u** and another undotted **u**.
- ihu (face) - This is a pairing between the undotted **i** and the undotted **u**.

Note: *E group vowels are also referred to as the "heavy vowel" group, because the vocal cords vibrate a lot when these vowels are pronounced.*

CHAPTER 2 UNIT 2 - SKILLS TEST

1. How many vowel groups are in the Igbo language?
    a. 3
    b. 2
    c. 1
    d. 4

2. What are these vowel groups called?

3. Which vowel group would **ọnwa** (moon) fall into?
    a. A group
    b. D group
    c. C group
    d. E group

4. What is another name for the A group?

5. What is another name for the E group?

6. Which vowel group would **enyi** (friend / elephant) fall into?
    a. D group
    b. O group
    c. E group

d. A group

7. Do you know the vowel harmony rules? Are you sure? Write them down.

Chapter Two
Unit Three

VOWEL HARMONY AND COMPOUND WORDS

When two words are combined to create a new meaning, the resulting word is called a **compound word**. In Unit 2, we talked about vowel harmony rules and how vowels from each group can only be paired with other vowels within their group. However, when it comes to creating compound words in Igbo, things are a little different.

Sometimes, each word being combined keeps its vowel harmony rule.

Example:

- ụlọ (house) + ala (floor / low) = ụlọ - ala (one story house)

However, there are instances in which a word from one vowel group can change to accommodate the vowel group of the other word it is being combined with.

Example:
- ọke (rat) + ụlọ (house) = oke - ulo (domestic rat). Notice that the dotted **u** and **o** in ụlọ (house) drop their dots.

Chapter Three
IGBO VOCABULARY + PARTS OF SPEECH

Now that you know the Igbo alphabet, next comes mastering Igbo vocabulary and parts of speech! Here's a list of common Igbo vocabulary words you'll use in conversation or should know just for fun. Some words might vary depending on dialect and the context in which they are used.

Tip: When memorizing Igbo vocabulary, it's best to start off with the words you are most likely to use in conversation. That being said, feel free to circle words you feel you would use the most!

COMMON PHRASES
Welcome - Nnọọ
Hello - Ndewo
How are you? - Kedu?
I am fine. - A dị m mma
Everything is fine. - Ọ dị mma
Yes - Ee
No - Mba
Please - Biko
Wait / Excuse me - Chere
Sorry - Ndo
Forgive me - Gbaghara m

Good night - Ka chi huo
Thank you - Daalụ
Thank you - Imeela
Safe journey - Ije ọma
See you next time! - Ka emesia
Good job - Jisie ike
Good luck - Ya di kwara gi mma
Leave me alone, please - Hapu m aka, biko
I don't want it - Achọghị m ya
I love you - A hụrụ m gị n'anya
My name is (insert name) - Aha m bụ (insert name)
I don't know - Amaghị m
I speak a little Igbo - A na m asụ Igbo ntakiri
I am from (insert place) - A bụ m onye (insert place)

FAMILY / PEOPLE
People - Ndi Mmadụ
Person - Mmadụ
Family / Clan - Ezi na ulo
Public - Ọha mmadụ
Child - Nwa
Children - Ụmụaka / Ụmụ
Daughter - Nwa Nwanyị
Son - Nwa Nwoke
Oldest Daughter - Ada
Oldest son - Di ọkpara
Mother - Nne
Father - Nna
Husband - Di
Wife - Nwunye

Grandmother - Nne nne / Mama nke ukwu
Grandfather - Nna nna / Papa nke ukwu
Woman - Nwanyị

Nwanyị

Man - Nwoke
Young Lady - Agbọghọbia
Young Man - Okorọbia
Student - Nwa akwụkwọ
Grandchild - Nwa nwa
In-law - Ọgọ

- **Sister in law** - Ọgọ m nwanyị
- **Brother in law** - Ọgọ m nwoke

- **Mother in law**:
  - Husband's mother: Nne di m
  - Wife's mother: Ọgọ m nwanyị / Nne nwunye m
- **Father in law**:
  - Husband's father: Nna di m
  - Wife's father: Ọgọ m nwoke/ Nna nwunye m

Parents - Nne na Nna
Baby - Nwata / Nwatakiri
Twins - Ụmụ ejima

Ụmụ ejima

Sibling (singular) / Relative/ Very close friend - Nwanne (depending on the context)

- Sister - Nwanne m nwanyị
- Brother - Nwanne m nwoke

Siblings (plural) / Relatives from your mother's side: Ụmụnne
Extended family / Father's side of the family: Ụmụnna

Niece / Nephew: Nwa nwanne m
- If your niece / nephew is from your sister, you say: *nwa nwanne m nwanyị*
- If your niece / nephew is from your brother, you say: *nwa nwanne m nwoke*

Friend(s) - Enyi / Ndi enyi (plural)
Girlfriend / Female friend - Enyi nwanyị
Boyfriend / Male friend - Enyi nwoke
Widow - Nwanyị isimkpe
Orphan - Nwa ogbenye
Mr. - Mazi
Mrs. - Odoziaku
Elders - Ndichie / Ndi okenye
Aunt / Older sister / Older female relative - Dada
Uncle / Older brother / Older male relative - Dede
Teacher / Professor - Onye nkuzi
Boss - Onye isi
Hairdresser - Onye na-edozi isi
Coworkers - Ndi ọrụ

HOUSEHOLD ITEMS
House / Home - Ụlọ

Backyard - Azu ụlọ
Inside (the house) / Room - Ime ụlọ
Door - Ụzọ
Floor / Ground - Ala
Chair - Oche
Pot - Ite
Soap - Ncha
Phone - Ekwe ntị

Ekwe ntị

Mirror - Enyo
Rug / Mat - Ute
Box - Igbe
Money - Ego

Book / Paper - Akwụkwọ
Bicycle - Igwe
Car - Ụgbọ ala
Cabinet - Okpokoro

TIME
Morning - Ụtụtụ
Afternoon - Ehihe
Early - N'oge
Evening / Night - Abalị / Anyasi
Hour - Elekere
Day - Ụbọchị
Week - Izu ụka
Month - Ọnwa
Year - Afọ
Time - Oge
Today - Taa
Tomorrow - Echi
Yesterday - Ụnyahụ
Now / Present - Ugbu a
Past - Oge gara aga
Future - Oge na abia
Forever - Ebighị ebi
Start - Mbido
End / Stop - Nkwusi

FOOD / EATING
Food - Nri
Breakfast - Nri ụtụtụ
Cup - Iko

Bottle - Kalama
Plate / bowl - Efere
Fork - Ngaji eze
Spoon - Ngaji
Knife - Mma
Lunch - Nri ehihe
Dinner - Nri abali
Drinks - Ihe ọṅụṅụ
Wine / Juice - Mmanya

Mmanya

Water - Mmịrị
Bread - Achịcha
Fruits - Mkpuru osisi
Vegetables - Akwụkwọ nri

Avocado - Ube bekee
Corn - Ọka
Coconut - Aki bekee
Mushroom - Ero
Yam - Ji
Fish - Azụ
Stockfish - Okporoko
Eggs - Akwa

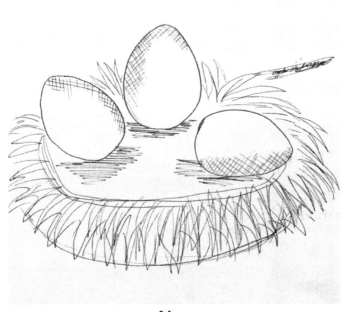

Akwa

Rice - Osikapa
Beans - Akidi / Agwa
Oil - Mmanụ
Pepper - Ose
Soup - Ofe

Meat - Anụ
Kola nut - Ọji
Salt - Nnu
Sugar - Nnu bekee
Hunger - Agụụ

THE BODY
Body / Skin - Ahụ
Hand - Aka
Right Hand - Aka nri
Left Hand - Aka ikpa / Aka ekpe
Finger - Mkpisi aka
Heart / Chest - Obi
Head - Isi
Hair - Ntụtụ isi
Mouth - Ọnụ
Lips - Egbugbere ọnụ
Nose - Imi
Neck - Olu
Teeth - Eze

Egbugbere ọnụ

Tongue - Ire
Throat - Akpịrị
Leg / Foot - Ụkwụ
Knees - Ikpere
Face - Ihu
Eye - Anya
Eyebrows - Iku anya
Ear - Ntị
Back - Azụ
Cheek - Nti
Belly button - Otuwe
Stomach - Afọ
Toes - Mkpisi ụkwụ
Waist - Ukwu
Clothes - Efe / Akwa
Bracelet - Mgba aka

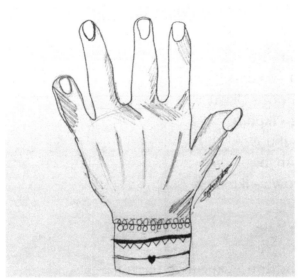

Mgba aka

Hat / Cap - Okpu
Bag / Purse - Akpa
Earrings - Ọla ntị
Necklace - Ihe olu
Jewelry - Ọla
Scarf / Headtie - Ichafu

PLACES / NATURE

School / Library - Ụlọ akwụkwọ
Church - Ụlọ ụka
Hospital - Ụlọ ọgwụ
Store / Market - Ahịa
Sky / Heaven - Elu igwe
Land - Ala
Seeds - Mkpuru

Hill / Mountain - Ugwu
Sun - Anwụ
Moon - Ọnwa

Ọnwa

Shade - Ndo
Fire - Ọkụ
Star - Kpakpando
Tree - Osisi
Rocks - Okwute
Stick(s) - Osisi
Dirt / Sand / Soil - Aja
Air - Ikuku
Wind - Ikuku
Chicken - Ọkụkọ
Goat - Ewu
Horse - Inyinya

Lamb / Sheep - Atụrụ
Pig - Ezi
Fish - Azụ
Rat / Mouse - Oke
Dog - Nkita
Elephant - Enyi

Enyi

Frog - Akiri
Toad - Awọ
Snake - Agwọ
Lizard - Ngwere
Fly - Ijiji
Ants - Ahụhụ
Mosquito - Anwụnta
Cockroach - Ochicha

MISCELLANEOUS
Thing / Something - Ihe

Language - Asụsụ
Thoughts - Echiche
Dance - Egwu
Music - Egwu
Play - Egwu
Fear - Egwu
Promise - Nkwa
Strength / Power - Ike
Lie(s) - Asi
Truth - Eziokwu
Song - Abụ
Peace - Udo
Work - Ọrụ
Dream - Nrọ
Love - Ịhụnanya
Prayer - Ekpere
English - Bekee
Life - Ndụ
Death - Ọnwụ
Word(s) - Okwu
King - Eze
Queen - Eze nwanyi
War - Agha
Faith - Okwukwe
Way / Journey - Ụzọ
Gift - Onyinye
Answer - Azịza
Protection - Nchedo
Blood - Ọbara
Medicine - Ọgwụ
Culture / Tradition - Omenala

Boat - Ụgbọ mmiri
Airplane - Ụgbọ elu
Wedding - Agbam akwụkwọ
Memory - Ncheta
Will / Purpose - Nzube
Wrongdoing / Sin - Mmehie
Forgiveness - Mgbaghara
Discussion - Nkata
Law / Fine - Iwu
Wisdom - Amamihe
Smile / Laugh - Ọchị
Cry - Akwa
Country - Obodo
Fight - Ọgụ
Gold - Ọla edo
Silver - Ọla ọcha

IGBO NUMBERS

The numbers I use are in standard Igbo, but there are various terms for certain numbers depending on dialect. Don't be alarmed if you're speaking Igbo and someone uses a different term!

Make sure that before you move on to learning bigger numbers, you have mastered numbers one through ten, as these are extremely important.

(1-10)
1 One - Otu
2 Two - Abụọ

3 Three - Ato
4 Four - Ano
5 Five - Ise
6 Six - Isii
7 Seven - Asaa
8 Eight - Asato
9 Nine - Itoolu
10 Ten - Iri

(11 - 19)
Remember when I said that you had to learn numbers 1-10 before moving on? Here's why: In Igbo, numbers from 11 - 19 are formed using this equation:

Iri (10) + "na" (and) + any number less than ten

For example, if you wanted to say *eleven*, eleven is equal to 10 plus 1 - meaning in Igbo, this would be iri na otu - which translates to "ten and one."

11 Eleven - Iri na otu
12 Twelve - Iri na abuo
13 Thirteen - Iri na ato
14 Fourteen - Iri na ano
15 Fifteen - Iri na ise
16 Sixteen - Iri na isii
17 Seventeen - Iri na asaa
18 Eighteen - Iri na asato
19 Nineteen - Iri na itoolu

(20 - 90)

Again, here's why numbers 1-10 are extremely important. If you want to talk about numbers made up of multiple compounds of 10, you use this equation:

Iri (10) + any number less than 10

For example, if you wanted to say **seventy,** which is 7 sets of 10, this would be iri asaa, which translates to "seven tens."

20 Twenty - Iri abụọ
30 Thirty - Iri atọ
40 Forty - Iri anọ
50 Fifty - Iri ise
60 Sixty - Iri isii
70 Seventy - Iri asaa
80 Eighty - Iri asatọ
90 Ninety - Iri itoolu

Keep in mind, do not use "na" when you're talking about numbers made of multiple sets of ten. Doing this would completely change the number! Iri asaa (70) **is drastically different from** iri na asaa (17).

Compounding Numbers Less than 100

If you understand the equations for creating numbers 11-19 and creating numbers that are multiples of 10 - this part should be a breeze for you! Let's say you want to talk about **eighty-four.** How would you do this?

Here's how: Combine the 11-19 equation with the multiples of 10 equation to get:

Iri (10) + number less than 10 + "na" (and) + another number less than 10

This looks confusing, but you can do it. We're just going to break apart the equation. So, to form *eighty-four*, this is what you would do:

1. Form the *eighty* part first. There are 8 tens in 80, so that is iri asatọ.
2. Now that you have eighty, what's left? *Four,* which is anọ.
3. Combine the two numbers you have using "na." So, eighty-four is iri asatọ na anọ.

(100 - 900)
100 in Igbo is nari. To talk about multiple hundreds up to 900, you just add a number from 2 - 9 after *nari*. In the case of one hundred, the "otu" goes before the *nari*.

100 one hundred - Otu nari
200 two hundred - Nari abụọ
300 three hundred - Nari atọ
400 four hundred - Nari anọ
500 five hundred - Nari ise
600 six hundred - Nari isii
700 seven hundred - Nari asaa
800 eight hundred - Nari asatọ

900 nine hundred - Nari itoolu

Compound Numbers 100 - 900:
Since you have learned how to compound numbers less than 100, this part should be a little bit easier. Let's say you want to talk about the number 153. This is what you would do:

1. Focus on the 100 part first, 100 is otu nari.
2. What do you have left? 53. Take that apart and do the *fifty* in Igbo first, which is iri ise.
3. Combine the 100 and the 50 using "na" (and), the same way you would if you were creating a compound number less than 100. This would give you *otu nari na iri ise,* which is 150.
4. Now, all you have left is 3, which is ato. Attach the 3 to the end of the 150 using "na." So, 153 in Igbo is *otu nari na iri ise na ato.*

(1,000 - 10,000)
1,000 in Igbo is puku. To talk about multiple thousands up to 10,000 - you just add a number from 2 - 10 after puku. In the case of one thousand, the "otu" goes before the puku.

1,000 one thousand - Otu puku
2,000 two thousand - Puku abuo
3,000 three thousand - Puku ato
4,000 four thousand - Puku ano
5,000 five thousand - Puku ise
6,000 six thousand - Puku isii

7,000 seven thousand - Puku asaa
8,000 eight thousand - Puku asatọ
9,000 nine thousand - Puku itoolu
10,000 ten thousand - Puku iri

- The rules for 11 - 19 and multiples of ten apply to the thousands as well. For example, if you wanted to say "eleven thousand," that would be puku iri na otu. If you wanted to say "seventy thousand," that would be puku iri asaa.

Compounding Numbers 1,000 - 10,000

The compounding rules for numbers 1,000 - 10,000 are the same as the ones we've gone through before, only you would use "na" much more frequently since the number you're creating is much larger. For example, if you wanted to say 4,984, this is what you would do:

1. Focus on the thousands first. There are four thousand, so this would be puku anọ.
2. Next, move on to the hundreds - there are nine of them, so you would say nari itoolu.
3. Then, you have the tens' place. There are eight tens in this number, so you would say iri asatọ.
4. All you have left is four, which is anọ.
5. Now, combine all the numbers you've created using "na." This would give you puku anọ na nari itoolu na iri asatọ na anọ.

Ordinal Numbers in Igbo

Ordinal numbers are numbers that describe the order of something in a sequence - like *first, second, third*. In Igbo, ordinal numbers are formed by putting the adjective "nke" in front of the number you are using to describe order in a sequence. The only exception to this is when you are talking about the FIRST thing in a sequence, *first* is nke mbụ.

Examples:
Second is nke abụọ.
Fifteenth is nke iri na ise.
Sixty eighth is nke iri isii na asatọ.
Eight hundredth is nke nari asatọ.
Seven thousandth is nke puku asaa.

SKILLS TEST - IGBO NUMBERS

1. How would you say *37* in Igbo?

2. How do you form compound numbers less than 100 in Igbo?

3. How would you say *168* in Igbo?

4. True or False: **Iri na asato** and **Iri asato** are the same number.

5. How would you say *seventeenth* in Igbo?

6. How would you say *seventy fifth* in Igbo?

7. Write these numbers in Igbo:

    - 56 -

- 148 -

- 79 -

- 93 -

- 831 -

- 1,477 -

- 3,232 -

NOUNS IN THE IGBO LANGUAGE

Nouns are words that refer to people, places, or things. The vocabulary lists you just looked through are full of nouns - from family members to animals. However, it doesn't end there! Here are a few rules you need to know on nouns in the Igbo language:

1. Plural Nouns

When we make a noun plural, it is because we're talking about more than one person, place, or thing. In English, we make nouns plural by adding an "s" or an "es" at the end of the word.

For example:

One cookie →Two cookies

One church →Five churches

In Igbo, plural nouns are spelled exactly the same way as singular nouns. This is both convenient and confusing because while you don't have to worry about adding an ending, you do have to rely on context to determine whether a noun is plural or singular.

However, if you want to emphasize that the nouns you are talking about are plural, you can place either **Ndį, Otųtų,** or **Umu** in front of them.

For example:

Agbọghọbia (young lady) →Umu agbọghọbia (young ladies)

Onye nkuzi (teacher) →Ndị nkuzi (teachers)

Nkita (dog)→Otụtụ nkita (dogs)

2. "Onye"

The word *onye* means **"one / person / someone (who)"** or **"doer of."** In Igbo, when you want to talk about a profession or a title, you put "onye" in front of a word that describes who that person is or what that person does.

For example:

Onye *na-edozi isi* → Someone who does hair (hairdresser).

Onye *Nigeria* → Someone from Nigeria (Nigerian).

Onye *nke m* →One of my own (someone you're very close to).

Onye *nkuzi* → Someone who teaches (teacher).

3. Nouns + Numbers

If you want to specify the number of nouns you are referring to, you can use numbers - especially now that you've learned up to 10,000!

In English, we specify the number of nouns by placing a number in front of the noun.

For example:
Five flowers
Twenty yards

Things are a little different in Igbo. When you want to use numbers to describe the amount of people, places, or things, **the number goes after the noun.**

For example:
Two trees = Osisi abụọ
Ten peppers = Ose iri
Fourteen men = Nwoke iri na anọ

There is one exception to the rule - and that is when you are talking about **one** of something. In Igbo, "One" (otu) always goes **in front of the noun.**

For example:
One hand = Otu aka
One tree = Otu osisi

4. Ordinal Numbers

In the "Igbo Numbers" section, we talked about ordinal numbers, which are numbers that describe the order of something in a sequence. When you want to use an ordinal number to describe the order of a noun in English, the number always goes in front.

For example:
First child
Second apple

Similar to the non-ordinal numbers, ordinal numbers **go after the noun** in the Igbo language. However, there is one difference. With ordinal numbers, you put **"nke"** before the number that goes after the noun.

For example:
Second tree = Osisi nke abụọ
Third book = Akwụkwọ nke atọ

There are no exceptions to this rule, but remember: *when you are talking about an item that comes **first**, you say **nke mbụ** not "nke otu."*

ADJECTIVES IN THE IGBO LANGUAGE

An adjective is a word that is used to describe a noun. In English, adjectives usually go before the noun they are describing.

For example:
Hot weather
Small girl

In Igbo, adjectives go **after the noun they are describing.**

For example:
Beautiful woman = Nwanyị ọma

Long throat = Akpịrị ogologo
Small book = Akwụkwọ ntakiri

Here is a list of common Igbo adjectives:

Sweet - Ụtọ
Small - Obere / Ntakiri
Big - Ukwu
Bitter - Ilu
Long - Ogologo
Short - Ntakiri
Bright - Ọcha
Clean - Ọcha
Dark - Oji
Beautiful - Ọma / Mma / Ọmarịcha
Good - Ọma
Ugly - Ọjọọ
Bad - Ọjọọ
Happy - Obi ụtọ / Añụri
Sad - Obi ọjọọ
Angry - Obi ọjọọ / Iwe
Shy - Ihere
Hot - Ọkụ
Cold - Oyi
Holy / Sacred - Nsọ
Close - Nso
Far - Anya
Hard - Siri ike
Expensive - Dara ọnụ
Empty - Chakoo
High - Elu

Low - Ala
New - Ọhụrụ
Old - Ochie / Agadi
Fast - Ọsịsọ / Ngwa ngwa

DEMONSTRATIVE ADJECTIVES

Demonstrative adjectives are used to clarify which nouns we are talking about. Here's a list of demonstrative adjectives in Igbo:

That - **Ahụ**
This - **Nke a**
Those - **Ndị ahu**
These - **Ndị a**

Demonstrative adjectives also go after the nouns they are describing.

For example:
These hands = Aka ndị a
That book = Akwụkwọ ahụ

PREPOSITIONS IN THE IGBO LANGUAGE

Prepositions are words that link nouns and pronouns to a verb or adjective within the same sentence. Prepositions can also be used to describe the location of things and sometimes the time that things occur. Examples of prepositions in English are *with, of, from, since,* and *across.*

Prepositions in the Igbo language are used the same way prepositions are used in English, meaning you can place them in the middle, the beginning, or the end of a sentence.

Here's a list of common prepositions in Igbo:

From - Site
For - Maka
Of - Nke
Inside - N'ime
Like / As - Dịka
Near - Nso
Up - N'elu
Down / Below - N'ala
With - Na
At - Na
On - Na
In front (of) - N'ihu
Beside - N'akụkụ
Behind - N'azụ
Between - N'etiti
Since - Ka mgbe
Until - Ruo
Above - N'elu
About - Gbasara
Before - Tupu
After - Emechaa
Underneath - N'okpuru

Igbo Prepositions Used in Sentences:

1. Chiamaka is coming **near**. → Chiamaka na-abịa **nso.**
2. Ugonna is **beside** Ifeanyi. → Ugonna nọ **n'akụkụ** Ifeanyi.
3. She is **inside** the house. → Ọ nọ **n'ime** ụlọ.

CONJUNCTIONS IN THE IGBO LANGUAGE

Conjunctions are used to connect words, phrases, or clauses. Examples of conjunctions in English are: *or, and, but,* and *so.*

Here's a list of commonly used conjunctions in Igbo:

And - Na
But - Ma / Mana
Except - E wezụga
So (that) - Ka ọ were
However - Mana
If - Ma
Instead - Kama
Even (if) - Ọbụrụgodu na
Or - Ma ọ bụ
Because / Due to the fact - Maka / N'ihi na
As - Dịka

Igbo Conjunctions Used in Sentences:

1. Izunna is eating, **but** Chidera is sleeping. →
Izunna na-eri nri, **mana** Chidera na-arahụ ụra.

2. **Even if** Chidera is sleeping, Izunna will eat. →
Ọbụrụgodu na Chidera na-arahụ ụra, Izunna ga-eri nri.

ADVERBS IN THE IGBO LANGUAGE

Adverbs are words that describe how, when, or where an action is done. The action can come in the form of a verb or an adjective. In English, examples of adverbs are *quickly, always,* and *slowly.*

In Igbo, adverbs can be used at the beginning or the end of a sentence; they don't usually appear in the middle of a sentence.

For example:
She ate today. →O riri nri taa.

Today, she ate. → Taa, o riri nri.

Here's a list of commonly used adverbs in Igbo:

Today - Taa
Tomorrow - Echi
Yesterday - Ụnyahụ
Always - Mgbe n'ile
Almost - Kwa / Obere ihe / Ọfọrọ ntakiri

Quickly - Ọsịsọ / Ngwa
Immediately - Ozugbo
Sometimes - Mgbe ụfọdụ
Only - Nanị / So
Soon - Ngwa ngwa / Mgbe n'adịghị anya
Slowly - Nwayọ / Nwayọ nwayọ (this adds more emphasis)
Again - Ọzọ
Together - Ọnụ
Well - Ọma / Ọfụma

Igbo Adverbs in Sentences:

1. Amarachi ate **quickly**. → Amarachi riri nri **ọsịsọ**.

2. It went **well**. → Ọ gara **ọfụma**.

3. **Sometimes**, she sleeps. → **Mgbe ụfọdụ**, ọ na-arahụ ụra.

PART TWO
FUNDAMENTALS OF IGBO GRAMMAR

Chapter Four
TONE MARKS

In Chapter 1, you learned that Igbo is a tonal language - meaning that it uses pitch to distinguish between words of the same spelling. Words that are spelled the same but have different meanings or pronunciations are called **homographs** in English. There are quite a few homographs in Igbo, so in order to ensure that you're properly expressing what you want to say, you can use tone marks.

Tone marks are typically placed above vowels and help differentiate between high tones, middle tones, and low tones in Igbo to show how a word is pronounced. However, they are not always used in written Igbo.

Tip: Listening to Igbo being spoken aloud helps with learning how to pronounce the different tones.

There are three types of tone marks in the Igbo language.

The first tone mark is called **Ụdaelu.** It is an accent mark that slants up from left to right (´). If you see this accent mark above a vowel in an Igbo word, that means the vowel is pronounced with a high-pitched tone.

The second tone mark is called **Ụdansuda.** It is typically marked with a symbol known as the circumflex (^). If you see the circumflex above a vowel in an Igbo word, that means the vowel is pronounced with a mid-tone.

The third tone mark is called **Ụdaala.** It is an accent mark that slants up from right to left (`). If you see this accent mark above a vowel in an Igbo word, that means the vowel is pronounced with a low tone.

For example:
Ézê (EH-ZEH) - Teeth
In this word, there is an **Ụdaelu** and an **Ụdansuda**, which means you would say the first E with a high tone, and the second e with a mid-tone.

Ézè (EH-ZEH) - King / Ruler
In this word, there is an **Ụdaelu** and an **Ụdaala,** which means you would say the first e with a high tone, and the second e with a low tone.

Practice: Below are other examples of homographs in Igbo. The locations of the accent marks are provided. To help you remember what each mark looks like, I want you to fill them in. You can do it!

1. *Akwa* - This word can mean *egg, cry, or cloth.*

Akwa (egg)
To make *akwa* mean *egg*, you would put an **Ụdaala on the first "A"** and an **Ụdaelu** on the second "A".

Akwa (cry)
To make *akwa* mean *cry*, you would put an **Ụdaelu on both the first "A" and the second "A"**.

Akwa (cloth)
To make *akwa* mean cloth, you would put an **Ụdaelu on the first "A"** and an **Ụdaala on the second "A"**.

2. *Egwu* - This word can mean *dance*, *play*, *music*, or *fear*.

Egwu (dance / play / music)
To make *egwu* mean *dance, play, or music,* you would put an **Ụdaelu on both the "E" and the "U"**. However, because this word has three potential meanings with the same pronunciation, the exact meaning of the word would be based on context.

Egwu (fear)
To make *egwu* mean *fear*, you would add an **Ụdaelu on the "E"** and an **Ụdaala on the "U"**.

Chapter Five
IGBO PRONOUNS

Pronouns are words used in place of nouns that can describe a broad range of nouns. In English, examples of pronouns include: *he, she, her,* and *it.* In Igbo, pronouns are not gender specific. This means the same pronouns can be used to describe anyone. In this chapter, we're going to talk about the different types of pronouns in the Igbo language.

FIRST PERSON PRONOUNS
These are pronouns that are used when the speaker is talking **about themselves or a group they are in**.

First person pronouns in English:

Me / I	We
This is me.	We are matching.
I am smiling.	

In Igbo, the first-person pronouns are:

- **m** *(I, me)*
- **mụ** *(I, me)*
- **anyị** *(we)*

Example:
I am coming to eat. → **M** na-abịa iri nri.

In this sentence, you would use **M** since the speaker is talking about themselves.

We are coming to eat. →**Anyị** na-abịa iri nri.

In this sentence, **Anyị** would be used because the use of *we* shows that the speaker is part of the group.

SECOND PERSON PRONOUNS

These are used when the speaker is talking **directly to someone or a group that the person they are speaking to is in.**

Second person pronouns in English:

You (singular)   You (plural)
You are wearing pearls.   You guys are listening.

In Igbo, the second person pronouns are:

- i / ị *(you)*
- gị *(you) *use depends on context*
- ụnụ *(you guys, plural)*

Example:

You are beautiful. → **Ị** mara mma.

In this sentence, **Ị** **would** be used since it is evident that speaker is talking directly to someone.

You guys are beautiful. → Ụnụ mara mma.

In this sentence, the speaker is talking directly to a group of people, which means Ụnụ would be used.

THIRD PERSON PRONOUNS

These are used when **someone or something is being talked about. They are also used when a group of people or things are being talked about.**

Third person pronouns in English:

He
He is talking.

She
She is the leader.

It
It is a phone.

They
They are dressed up.

In Igbo, the third person pronouns are:

- **o / ọ** *(she, he, it)*
- **ya** *(her, him, it)*
- **ha** *(they, them)*

Example:

Ifeanyi is going to school. → Ọ na-aga ụlọ akwụkwọ.

The speaker is talking about someone, which means that Ọ would be used. This is because if you were to replace Ifeanyi with a pronoun, the pronouns you could use are *he* or *she*.

Chinemerem and Izunna are going to school.

→ **Ha** na-aga ụlọ akwụkwọ.

If you were to replace Chinemerem and Izunna with a pronoun, the pronoun you would use is *they*. In Igbo, you would use **Ha.**

POSSESSIVE PRONOUNS

These are pronouns that **demonstrate ownership** in a sentence. Possessive pronouns in the Igbo language are:

- **m / mụ** *(mine)*
- **gị** *(yours)*
- **ụnụ** *(yours - plural)*
- **ya** *(hers, his, its)*
- **ha** *(theirs)*
- **anyị** *(ours)*

Whenever you use a possessive pronoun, you always put the word *nke* in front of it.

Example:

That book is Onyeka's. → Akwụkwọ ahụ bụ **nke ya.**

The book belongs to Onyeka, who is being talked about. Therefore, you would use **nke ya** to replace Onyeka in this sentence.

That book is yours. →Akwụkwọ ahụ bụ **nke gị.**

The speaker is talking directly to someone, which means you would use **nke gị** in this sentence.

DEMONSTRATIVE PRONOUNS

These are pronouns that point to specific things. Guess what? You already know most of them! Remember the demonstrative adjectives we talked about in Chapter 3? A lot of the demonstrative pronouns are the same words. In Igbo, the demonstrative pronouns are:

- That - **ahụ**
- This - **nke a**
- Those - **ndị ahụ**
- These - **ndị a**

Example:

I want these, please. → A chọrọ m **ndị a,** biko.

In this sentence, **ndị a** would be used since the speaker wants *these*.

Give me those. → Nye m **ndị ahụ.**

In this sentence, **ndị ahu** would be used since the speaker is asking for *those*.

INTERROGATIVE PRONOUNS

Interrogative pronouns are used when you want to ask a question about someone or something. In Igbo, they are:

- What? - **Gịnị?**
- Where? - **Ebee?**
- Why? - **Maka gịnị?**
- How? - **Kedu?**
- When? - **Olee Mgbe?**
- Who? - **Onye?**
- Which? - **Olee?**

Examples:

Who is that woman? → **Onye** bụ nwanyị ahụ?

This question is asking about a person, hence the use of the interrogative pronoun *Who*. In Igbo, you would use **Onye**.

What is that thing? → **Gịnị** bụ ihe ahụ?

The question is asking *What*, which means you would use **Gịnị**.

Subject vs. Object Pronoun Use

When it comes to singular pronouns, you might notice that there are multiple pronouns that can be used to describe the same person or thing. However, these seemingly similar pronouns cannot be used interchangeably. They depend on whether the person or thing being talked about is the subject or the object of a sentence.

SUBJECT PRONOUNS

These are pronouns that usually only replace the subject of a sentence; the person or thing **doing the action**. In Igbo, the singular subject pronouns are:
- **m** *(I)*
- **i / į** *(you)*
- **o / ọ** *(she, he, it)*

Examples:

She wants to eat. → Ọ chọrọ iri nri.

If you were to say this sentence in Igbo, you would have to use the pronoun **O / Ọ** to describe *she* because *she* is the subject of the sentence.

You are going home. → I na-ala ụlọ.

The pronoun **I / Į** would be used to replace *you* since *you* is the subject of the sentence.

The plural subject pronouns in Igbo are:
- **ha** *(they)*
- **anyį** *(we)*
- **ụnụ** *(you plural)*

Example:

We want to eat. → Anyị chọrọ iri nri.

In this sentence, you would use **Anyị** because *we* is the subject of the sentence.

OBJECT PRONOUNS

These are pronouns that usually replace the object of a sentence. The object is the person or thing **receiving the action.** In Igbo, the singular object pronouns are:

- **gị** *(you)*
- **ya** *(her, him, it)*
- **m / mụ** *(me)*

Examples:

Onyeka gave her the rice. → Onyeka nyere **ya** osikapa.

Since *her* is the object of the sentence, you would use **ya.**

She gave you the rice. → O nyere **gị** osikapa.

You is the object of this sentence, so you would use **gị.**

The plural object pronouns in Igbo are:
- **ha** *(them)*
- **anyị** *(us)*
- **ụnụ** *(you plural)*

Example:
> Onyeka gave them the rice. → Onyeka nyere ha osikapa.
> Since *them* is the object of the sentence, you would use **ha**.

Pronouns and Vowel Harmony

As you probably saw in the first part of this chapter, some pronouns in the Igbo language have dotted counterparts. These pronouns are:

- **O / Ọ** *(she, he, it)*
- **I / Ị** *(you)*

In Chapter 2 Unit 2, we talked about vowel harmony in the Igbo language, which is the pairing of vowels from the same vowel group. To review, the vowel groups in the Igbo language are the A group (**A, Ị, Ọ, Ụ**) and the E group (**E, I, O, U**).

Vowel harmony is what differentiates between a dotted pronoun and an undotted pronoun. How? The pronoun you use depends on whether or not the verb in the sentence fits into the A group or the E group.

Examples:
> Ọ gara iri nri. *(He / She / It went to eat.)* In this sentence, you would use the dotted O to talk

about *he / she / it* because the verb *gara* belongs in the A (dotted vowel) group.

> **I nwere efe.** *(You have clothes.)* In this sentence, you would use the undotted I because the verb *nwere* belongs in the E (undotted) vowel group.

CHAPTER 5 SKILLS TEST

1. How does **vowel harmony** affect pronoun use?

2. What are **third person pronouns**? Name the Igbo third person pronouns.

3. Circle the **second person** pronouns in this set of pronouns:
    a. ụnụ
    b. gị
    c. ha
    d. m

4. What are the types of pronouns talked about in this chapter?

5. What is the meaning of the Igbo pronoun *anyị*?
    a. Her
    b. She
    c. Me
    d. We

6. What is the difference between *ha* and *ya*?

7. *Maka gịnị?* means:
   a. Why?
   b. Who?
   c. Where?
   d. When?

8. Which of these is an example of a **possessive pronoun in Igbo**?
   a. Ya
   b. Ebee?
   c. Hers
   d. His

9. Do you know the Igbo pronoun rules? Go over them one more time.

CUMULATIVE SKILLS TEST: CHAPTERS 1 - 5

1. How many vowel groups are in the Igbo language? What are they called?

2. You're talking to your friend Adanna about school. Which Igbo pronouns would you use if you're speaking directly to her?

3. How many letters are in the Igbo Alphabet?

4. What is another name for the Igbo Alphabet?

5. Which of these is an example of a demonstrative pronoun?
    a. Ahụ
    b. Gịnị?
    c. Ya
    d. M

6. What are the vowels in the Igbo Alphabet? What is another name for Igbo vowels?

7. Which vowel group does the word Nne (mother) belong to?
    a. A group
    b. D group
    c. E group
    d. N group

8. Circle the first-person pronouns:
    a. M
    b. Ụnụ
    c. Ha
    d. Ya
    e. Anyị
    f. Ebee?

9. What are the vowel harmony rules in the Igbo language?

10. How many states are in Igboland?

11. What family of languages does Igbo fall into? What is a key characteristic of this language family?

12. How many consonants are in the Igbo language?
    a. 23

b. 24
c. 25
d. 28

13. How many Igbo letters are in efe?

14. True or False: Double consonants in the Igbo Alphabet are counted as two separate letters.

15. True or False: A group vowels should always be paired with E group vowels.

16. Identify the object pronoun in this sentence: I gave her the cookie.
    a. Him
    b. I
    c. Her
    d. Cookie

17. Regarding the question 17, which Igbo pronoun would you use to replace the object pronoun you identified?
    a. Ya
    b. M
    c. Ha
    d. Anyị

18. In what part of Nigeria is Igboland located?

19. Write the following numbers in Igbo:
- 86:
- 43:
- 194:
- 221:
- 546:
- 1,341:
- 3,987:

20. What are the names of the three tone marks in the Igbo language?

21. True or False: In Igbo, adjectives go after the word they are describing.

22. True or False: In Igbo, ordinal numbers go before the noun they are describing.

23. Write down 10 of your favorite Igbo words / phrases.

Chapter Six
VERBS, TENSES, COMMANDS, AND NEGATIONS

At this point, you know all about the Igbo alphabet, vowel harmony, and pronouns. Give yourself a pat on the back for making it this far! Now, let me tell you ahead of time that this chapter is going to be the MOST important chapter you need to learn in order to grasp the Igbo language. Grab a pencil, pen, or highlighter and get ready to master verbs, tenses, commands, and negations!

Before you read this chapter, it would be a good idea to go back to Chapter 2 and look over the Igbo alphabet. Doing this will help you remember the sounds of each letter, and knowing the sounds will help you with your pronunciation. I also recommend you look back at the vowel harmony rules from Chapter 2. Make sure you know your pronouns from Chapter 5, too!

VERBS IN THE IGBO LANGUAGE
Verbs are words used to indicate action. In English, the simplest form of a verb is the *infinitive form,* which is the word "to" in front of the verb.

For example:
To dance
To laugh
To be

In Igbo, the infinitive form of a verb is the letter **i / ị + the root of the verb.** Whether you use the dotted or undotted "i" is dependent on the vowel harmony of the verb root. If a verb root falls under the A group, then it is preceded by **ị** (dotted i). If a verb root falls under the E group, then it is preceded by **i** (undotted i).

For example:
To give - Inye
In this example, "nye" is the verb root meaning "give." To make it an infinitive, we add "I" (the undotted I) because "nye" falls under the E vowel group.

To come - Ịbịa
In this example, "bịa" is the verb root meaning "come." To make it an infinitive, we add "Ị" (the dotted I) because "bịa" falls under the A vowel group.

Here's a list of commonly used verbs in the Igbo language, in the infinitive form:

To be - Ịbụ / Ịdị
To come - Ịbịa
To stay / To be (at a location) - Ịnọ
To enter - Ịbata
To wear (clothes) - Iyi (efe)

To get out - Iputa
To leave - Ihapu
To eat (food) - Iri (nri)
To hear - Inu
To work - Iru oru
To tell - Igwa
To speak - Isu
To say - Ikwu
To take - Iwere
To see - Ihu
To look - Ile
To read - Igu
To want / To look for - Icho
To throw - Itu
To laugh - Ichi ochi
To bring - Iwete
To call - Ikpo
To follow - Isoro
To buy - Izuta
To sell - Ire
To get - Inweta
To give - Inye
To forget - Ichefu
To remember - Icheta
To write - Ide
To teach - Ikuzi
To do / make - Ime
To cry - Ibe akwa
To run - Igba oso
To think - Iche echiche
To walk - Iga ije

To go - Ịga
To hold - Ijide
To own / have - Inwe
To pray - Ikpe ekpere
To know - Ịma
To listen - Ige ntị
To sit - Ịnọdụ
To stand - Ikuli / Iguzo
To touch - Ịmetụ aka
To mark - Ịka
To sleep - Ịrahụ ụra
To bathe / take a shower - Ịsa ahụ
To sing (a song) - Ibu abụ / Ikwe ukwe
To play - Igwu egwu
To drink - Iṅụ
To dance - Ịgba egwu
To cook (food) - Isi nri
To fry - Ighe
To learn - Ịmụta
To chew - Ịta
To swallow - Ilo
To wash - Ịsa
To wait - Ichere
To understand - Ịghọta
To find out - Ịchọpụta

PRESENT TENSE

Present tense verbs describe an action that is currently occurring. The first present verb tense we'll be talking about is the **present simple tense**, which is used when an action occurs regularly.

Examples of the present simple tense in English:

I cook.
She sleeps.

For some verbs in Igbo, to create the present simple tense, you take off the **i / ị** that is in front of the infinitive, keeping the verb root. Then, you may add a pronoun in front depending on who or what you're talking about.

For example:

She knows. → Ọ ma.

"To know" in Igbo is **Ịma.** To conjugate the verb **Ịma** into the present simple tense, you drop the dotted i, which gives you the verb root ma. Then, you add in the pronoun. In this sentence, the pronoun is **she,** which in Igbo is **O / Ọ. Ịma** falls under the A vowel group, so you use the dotted O as the pronoun.

You are. → Ị bụ.

"To be" in Igbo is **Ịbụ.** To conjugate **Ịbụ** into the present simple tense, you drop the dotted i, which leaves you with the verb root bụ. Then you add in the pronoun. In this case, the pronoun is **you,** which in Igbo is **I / Ị.** Although there isn't an "A" or an "E" in the word **Ịbụ,** you can still determine that **Ịbụ** belongs in the A group because it has dotted I and a dotted U - meaning you use the dotted I as the pronoun.

Not every Igbo verb follows this rule exactly, though. From the list of infinitive verbs I've provided you with, the verbs that follow the "dropped I / Ị" rule are:

To be - Ịbụ
To know - Ima
To stay / To be (at a location) - Ịnọ
To wear (clothes) - Iyi efe

There are verbs that follow the "dropped I / Ị" rule, but require one extra step, which is adding an ending to the verb root.

If the verb root ends with an **o / ọ**, the corresponding ending is **-ro / rọ**.
If the verb root ends with an **e,** the corresponding ending is **-re.**
If the verb root ends with an **a,** the corresponding ending is **-ra.**
If the verb root ends with a **u / ụ**, the corresponding ending is **ru / rụ.**
If the verb root ends with a **i / ị,** the corresponding ending is **-ri / -rị.**

For example:

They want. → Ha chọrọ.

"To want" in Igbo is **Ịchọ**. First, you drop the dotted i from **Ịchọ,** which gives you the verb root chọ. Then, you add the corresponding ending to the verb root -

since chọ ends with a *dotted o*, the corresponding ending is -rọ. After adding the corresponding ending, you now have chọrọ. Next, you add the pronoun, which in this sentence is **they. They** in Igbo is *Ha.*

She has. → O nwere.

"To have" in Igbo is **Inwe.** First, you drop the undotted i from **Inwe,** which leaves you with the verb root nwe. Then, you add the corresponding ending to the verb root - since nwe ends with an *e*, the corresponding ending is **-re.** After you add the ending, then you have nwere. Next, you add the pronoun, which in this sentence is **she.** In Igbo, **she** is O / Ọ. Nwere falls under the E vowel group, so you use the undotted O as the pronoun.

Similar to the "dropped I / Ị" rule, only a few verbs use this rule. From the list of infinitive verbs I provided you with, the only verbs that follow the "dropped I / Ị + extra ending" rule are:

To want / To look for - Ịchọ
To see - Ịhụ
To own / have - Inwe

To conjugate all the other verbs on the list of infinitives into the present simple tense, you use the same rules as the present progressive tense.

The next present verb tense we'll be talking about is the **present progressive tense**, which is used when you want to talk about continuing action or an action that will happen in the future. In English, the present progressive is created by adding -*ing* to the end of a verb.

For example:

She is playing.
They are eating.

The present progressive tense in the Igbo language is very special. Remember the present simple tense? A majority of Igbo verbs use the same conjugation for **both the present simple and present progressive** tenses. So, the same way you would say "I am eating" in Igbo, you could also say, "I eat."

The present progressive tense is formed with these steps:

1. Drop the **i / ị** from the front of the infinitive form of the verb.

2. Replace the **i / ị** with an **"a"** or an **"e"** depending on vowel harmony. If the verb root falls under the A vowel group, you replace the **ị** from the infinitive form with an **a**. If the verb root falls under the E vowel group, then you replace the **i** from the infinitive form with an **e**.

3. Now, you add **"na - (na + hyphen)"** in front of your newly conjugated verb root. "Na" is a helping verb. Helping verbs are used alongside

a main verb to specify which tense is being used or whether a question is being asked.

Examples of present progressive in Igbo:

She is going to school. → Ọ na-aga ulọ akwụkwọ.

"To go" in Igbo is **ịga**. The first thing you do is drop the dotted i, which gives you the verb root ga. Ga belongs to the A vowel group, so you replace the dotted i with an "a." This now gives you aga. Next, you add the **na-** in front of your new verb root, which gives you na-aga. Lastly, you add the pronoun, which in this sentence is **she**. "She" in Igbo is O / Ọ, but you use the dotted O as the pronoun since na-aga belongs to the A vowel group.

> *This sentence could also mean ***"She goes to school,"*** so you would have to rely on context. If you want, you could add **ugbu a** (now) to the end of the sentence to emphasize that you are referring to an action that is currently happening.

> Ọ na-aga ulọ akwụkwọ ugbu a. → She is going to school right now.

Let's try another example:

Izunna is praying. → Izunna na-ekpe ekpere.

"To pray" in Igbo is **Ikpe ekpere**. The first thing you do is drop the undotted i, which gives you the verb root kpe ekpere. Kpe ekpere belongs to the E vowel group, so you replace the undotted i with an "e." This now gives you ekpe ekpere. Next, you add **na-**, which gives you na-ekpe ekpere. There is no pronoun in this sentence.

*This sentence could also mean *"Izunna prays,"* so if you wanted to emphasize that Izunna is currently praying, you could add **ugbu a** (now).

Izunna na-ekpe ekpere **ugbu a**. → Izunna is praying right now.

If you're using the present progressive form with the pronoun **M** to talk about yourself, there is an extra step. Regardless of whether the verb root falls under the A or E group, you must add "A" in front of the **na.** Instead of putting a hyphen after **na** in front of the conjugated verb root, you would place the **m** *in between the na and the verb root.* I know this looks confusing, so let's try an example:

I am praying. → A na m ekpe ekpere.

Notice that the infinitive form of **Ikpe ekpere** has been conjugated to **na - ekpe ekpere**. However, because you are using the pronoun **m,** you place **"A"** in front of **na**, remove the hyphen from **na - ekpe ekpere,** and place **m** in between "na" and "ekpe ekpere."

Not every dialect of Igbo uses this extra step, so it is perfectly acceptable if you choose not to use it. For example, you would still be understood if you left the **M** in front of the sentence the same way you would with every other pronoun. Like this:

M na-ekpe ekpere. → I am praying.

This also applies to the future tense.

VOWEL DROPPING

When you pronounce a present tense verb preceded by **"na,"** you have to mentally drop vowels when saying it aloud.

For example:

If you were to say **na-asụ** *(speaks / is speaking)*, you would pronounce it as **NAH - SOO,** even though it looks like it would be pronounced as **NAH - AH - SOO**. This is because you have to drop the "a" sound from **na.**

Let's do another example:

If you were to say **na-ekwu** *(says / is saying)*, it would be pronounced as **NEH - KWOO**, even though it looks like it would be pronounced as **NAH - EH - KWOO**. This is because you have to drop the "a" sound from **na**.

COMMANDS

We use commands when we want to instruct someone or request something.

Examples of commands in English:

Go!
Eat, please.
Leave it!

Forming commands in Igbo is much easier than forming the present tenses you just learned about, trust me. To create commands in Igbo, you drop the I / Ị from the infinitive form of the verb. That's it. Simple, right? Let's do some examples:

Go! → Ga!

"To go" in Igbo is **Ịga**. To form the command, you drop the dotted i, which leaves you with ga.

Leave! → Hapụ!

"To leave" in Igbo is **Ịhapụ**. To form the command, you drop the dotted i, which leaves you with hapụ.

Pray. → Kpe ekpere.

"To pray" in Igbo is **Ikpe ekpere.** To form the command, you drop the undotted i, which leaves you with kpe ekpere.

You can add nouns or pronouns if you want to specify your command. Nouns, like names, can go before or after a command, but the position of a noun can change the meaning of a command.

For example:

Onyeka, chere.
This command comes from the Igbo word **Ichere**, which means "to wait." In this sentence, you would be telling Onyeka to wait.

Chere Onyeka.
In this sentence, you would be commanding someone else to wait for Onyeka.

Pronouns always go after a command.

For example:

Leave us! → Hapụ anyị!
In this sentence, the first-person pronoun anyị goes after the command.

Write this. → Dee nke a.
In this sentence, the demonstrative pronoun **nke a** goes after the command.

PAST TENSE

We use the past tense of a verb when we want to talk about an action that already took place.

For example:

He cried.
They prayed.
She left.

In Igbo, the past tense is formed by dropping the I / Ị from the infinitive form of the verb, and adding a corresponding ending. The corresponding ending depends on the last letter of the verb root.

Guess what? You saw these endings when you learned the present simple tense!

If the last letter of a verb root is **o / ọ**, the corresponding ending is **-ro / rọ**.
If the last letter of a verb root is **e**, the corresponding ending is **-re**.
If the last letter of a verb root is **a**, the corresponding ending is **-ra**.
If the last letter of a verb root is **u / ụ**, the corresponding ending is **ru / rụ**.
If the last letter of a verb root is **i / ị**, the corresponding ending is **-ri / -rị**.

The vowel harmony of a verb determines if you use the dotted or undotted corresponding ending. If the last letter of a verb root is **ọ / ụ / ị**, it falls under the A vowel group. This means you use the dotted corresponding ending.

If the last letter of a verb root is **o / u / i,** it falls under the E vowel group. This means you use the undotted corresponding ending.

Let's do some examples:

Chinemerem danced. → Chinemerem gbara egwu.

"To dance" in Igbo is **Ịgba egwu.** To form the past tense, you drop the dotted i, which leaves you with gba. Since the last letter of this verb root is "a," the corresponding ending is -ra. Adding the corresponding ending gives you gbara egwu.

Ifeanyi wrote. → Ifeanyi dere.

"Wrote" is the past tense of "write," and "to write" in Igbo is **Ide.** To form the past tense, you drop the undotted I, which leaves you with de. Since the last letter of this verb root is e, the corresponding ending is -re. Adding the corresponding ending gives you dere.

Onyeka taught. → Onyeka kuziri.

"Taught" is the past tense of "teach," and "to teach" in Igbo is **Ikuzi**. To form the past tense, you drop the undotted I, which leaves you with kuzi. The last letter of this verb root is i and the i is undotted, meaning that kuzi falls under the E vowel group. Therefore, the

107

corresponding ending is -ri. Adding the corresponding ending gives you kuziri.

There are a few verbs that don't follow the past tense rule. These verbs are changed into the past tense simply by dropping the I / Ị from the infinitive form and keeping the verb root as is. On the list of infinitives at the beginning of this chapter, these irregular verbs are:

To be - Ịbụ / Ịdị
To follow - Isoro
To wait - Ichere

For example:

Chinemerem followed Onyeka yesterday. →

Chinemerem soro Onyeka ụnyahụ.

"To follow" in Igbo is **Isoro**. Since **Isoro** is an irregular verb in the past tense, all we have to do is drop the undotted I, which gives you soro.

Tip: If you want to specify that you are talking about the past when using these verbs, you can add a time period. In the example above, I used "yesterday," which is ụnyahụ.

FUTURE TENSE

We use the future tense when we want to talk about something that is going to happen or hasn't happened yet.

The future tense in Igbo is formed with these steps:

1. Drop the **i / ị** from the front of the infinitive form of the verb.

2. Replace the **i / ị** with an **"a"** or an **"e"** depending on vowel harmony. If the verb root falls under the A vowel group, you replace the **ị** from the infinitive form with an **a.** If the verb root falls under the E vowel group, then you replace the **i** from the infinitive form with an **e.**

3. Now, you add **"ga - (ga + hyphen)"** in front of your newly conjugated verb root. "Ga" is a helping verb. Helping verbs are used alongside a main verb to specify which tense is being used or whether a question is being asked.
Essentially, you're doing exactly the same thing you did with the present progressive tense. Only this time, instead of **na-,** you are adding **ga-** in front of the conjugated verb root.

Let's do some examples:

Chinemerem will eat. → Chinemerem ga-eri nri.

"To eat" in Igbo is **Iri**. The first thing you do is drop the undotted i, which gives you the verb root ri nri. Ri nri belongs to the E vowel group, so you replace the undotted i with an "e." This now gives you eri nri. Next, you add **ga-**, which gives you ga-eri nri.

Ifeanyi will go. → Ifeanyi ga-aga.

"To go" in Igbo is **ịga**. The first thing you do is drop the dotted i, which gives you the verb root ga. Ga belongs to the A vowel group, so you replace the dotted i with an "a." This now gives you aga. Next, you add the **ga-** in front of your new verb root, which gives you ga-aga.

The vowel dropping rules you learned from the present progressive tense also apply to the future tense. For example, **ga-aga** *(will go),* would be pronounced **GAH - GAH** instead of **GAH-AH-GA**. This is because you have to drop the "a" sound from **ga.**

Similar to the present progressive tense, if you're using the future tense with the pronoun *M* to talk about yourself, there is an extra step. Regardless of whether the verb root falls under the A or E group, you must add "A" in front of the **ga.** Instead of putting a hyphen after **ga** in front of the conjugated verb root, you would place the **m** *in between the ga and the verb root.*

For example:

I will go. → A ga m aga.

In this example, the infinitive form of **ịga** has been conjugated to **ga-aga**. However, because you are using the pronoun **m,** you place **"A"** in front of **ga**, remove the hyphen from **ga-aga,** and place **m** in between "ga" and "aga."

Once again, not every dialect of Igbo uses this extra step, so it is perfectly acceptable if you choose not to use it. For example, you would still be understood if you left the **M** in front of the sentence the same way you would with every other pronoun. Like this:

M ga-aga. → I will go.

NEGATIONS

We use negative verbs when we are talking about an action that does not happen, did not happen, or will not happen.

For example:
I am not Izunna.
He will not go.

Negations in the Present Simple Tense

For some negative verbs in the present simple tense in Igbo, you drop the I / Ị from the infinitive verb form and add **- ghi / - ghị** to the end of the verb root. Whether you use -ghi / -ghị is dependent on vowel harmony. If the verb root belongs to the A vowel group, you use the -ghị ending. If the verb root belongs to the E vowel group, then you use the -ghi ending. After adding the ending, you place an **"a"** in front of the verb that is negated if the verb root is part of the A vowel group, or an **"e"** if the verb is a part of the E vowel group.

Example:

Ifeanyi doesn't want food. → Ifeanyi achọghị nri.

"To want" in Igbo is **Ịchọ**. First, you drop the dotted i from Ịchọ, which leaves you with the verb root chọ. Because chọ has a dotted vowel, it belongs to the A vowel group. This means that you add the -ghị ending to chọ, which then gives you chọghị. Lastly, add an "a" in front of chọghị to get achọghị.

Ifeanyi doesn't have food. → Ifeanyi enweghi nri.

"To have" in Igbo is **Inwe**. First, you drop the undotted i from Inwe, which leaves you with the verb root nwe. Because nwe has an undotted vowel, it belongs to the E vowel group. This means that you add the -ghi ending to nwe, which then gives you nweghi. Lastly, add an "e" in front of nweghi to get enweghi.

If there is a pronoun at the beginning of a sentence with a negated verb in the present simple tense, then there is no need to add an "a" or "e" in front of the negated verb. The only exception to this rule is the pronoun "**m**." In the case of "m," the **"a / e" remains in front of the negated verb, and "m" comes after the negated verb.**

Example:

He doesn't want food. → Ọ chọghị nri.

The pronoun in this sentence is **he.** Since choghị falls under the A vowel group, you use the dotted o. Notice that because there is a pronoun in this sentence, there isn't an "a" in front of choghị.

I don't want food. → Achoghị m nri.

Since the pronoun m is in this sentence, you keep the "a" in achoghị and add **m** after achoghị to get achoghị m.

He doesn't have food. → O nweghi nri.

The pronoun in this sentence is **he.** Since nweghi falls under the E vowel group, you use the undotted o. Notice that because there is a pronoun in this sentence, there isn't an "e" in front of nweghi.

I don't have food. → Enweghi m nri.

Since the pronoun m is in this sentence, you keep the "e" in enweghi and add **m** after enweghi to get enweghi m.

On the list of infinitive verbs I provided you with, the only verbs that follow the "dropped I / Ị + -ghi / -ghị" rule in the present tense are:

To be - Ịbụ / Ịdị
To know - Ịma
To want / To look for - Ịcho

To stay / To be (at a location) - Ịnọ
To wear (clothes) - Iyi efe
To own / have - Inwe

The other verbs on the list follow the present progressive negation rule if they are being negated in present tense.

Negations in the Past Tense

To make verbs negative in the past tense, you use the same rules for the present simple tense - drop the I / Ị from the infinitive verb form and add - ghi / - ghị to the end of the verb root. Once again, whether you use -ghi / -ghị is dependent on vowel harmony. If the verb root belongs to the A vowel group, you use the -ghị ending. If the verb root belongs to the E vowel group, then you use the -ghi ending. After adding the ending, you place "a / e" in front of the verb that is negated depending on the vowel harmony of the verb root.

Example:

Onyeka didn't chew. → Onyeka ataghị.

"To chew" in Igbo is **Ịta**. First, you drop the dotted i from Ịta, which leaves you with the verb root ta. Ta belongs to the A vowel group. This means that you add the -ghị ending to ta, which then gives you taghị. Lastly, add an "a" in front of taghị (because it falls under the A vowel group) to get ataghị.

Nwando did not think. → Nwando echeghi echiche.

"To think" in Igbo is **Iche echiche**. First, you drop the undotted i from **Iche echiche,** which leaves you with the verb root che echiche. Che echiche belongs to the E vowel group. This means that you add the -ghi ending to che echiche, which gives you cheghi echiche. Lastly, because cheghi echiche falls under the E vowel group, you add an "e" in front of cheghi echiche to get echeghi echiche.

Just like the present simple tense, if there is a pronoun at the beginning of a sentence with a negated verb in the past tense, then there is no need to add an "a / e" in front of the negated verb. The only exception to this rule is the pronoun "m." In the case of "m," **the "a / e" remains in front of the negated verb, and "m" comes after the negated verb.**

She didn't chew. → Ọ taghị.

The pronoun in this sentence is **she.** Since taghị falls under the A vowel group, you use the dotted o. Notice that because there is a pronoun in this sentence, there isn't an "a" in front of taghị.

I didn't chew. → Ataghị m.

Since the pronoun m is in this sentence, you keep the "a" in ataghị and add **m** after ataghị to get ataghị m.

He didn't think. → O cheghi echiche.

The pronoun in this sentence is **he**. Since cheghi echiche falls under the E vowel group, you use the undotted o. Notice that because there is a pronoun in this sentence, there isn't an "e" in front of cheghi.

I didn't think. → Echeghi m echiche.

Since the pronoun m is in this sentence, you keep the "e" in echeghi echiche and add **m** after echeghi echiche to get echeghi m echiche. Whenever you have a verb that has two words, "m" always goes behind the part that has the - ghi / - ghị ending.

All verbs on the list follow the past tense negation rules.

Negations in the Present Progressive and Future Tenses

When negating Igbo verbs in the present tense, a majority of them are negated in present progressive form. To make a verb negative in the present progressive tense, you first conjugate the infinitive form of the verb into the present progressive tense using the steps you learned earlier. Next, you **add - ghị at the end of "na-,"** since "na" falls under the A vowel group. The conjugated verb root comes after. You then add an **"a"** in front of **"na-."**

For example:
Izunna is not eating. → Izunna anaghị eri nri.

"To eat" in Igbo is **Iri nri**. To change this into the negated present progressive tense, you take these steps:

Step 1: Conjugate **Iri nri** into the present progressive tense. This gives you **na-eri nri**.

Step 2: Take the hyphen away from **na-eri nri** and add **ghị** at the end. You now have **naghị eri nri**.

Step 3: Lastly, you put an "a" in front of **naghị eri nri**. This gives you anaghị eri nri.

Tip: Keep in mind that this sentence could also mean *"Izunna does not eat."* So, if you wanted to emphasize that Izunna is currently not eating, then you could add **ugbu a (now)** to the end of the sentence.

Izunna **anaghị eri nri** ugbu a. → Izunna is not eating *right now*.

If there is a pronoun at the beginning of a sentence with a negated verb in the present progressive tense, then you don't place "a" in front of **naghị**.

For example:

He is not eating. → Ọ naghị eri nri.

The pronoun in this sentence is **he**. Since naghị falls under the A vowel group, you use the dotted o. Notice that because there is a pronoun in this sentence, there isn't an "a" in front of naghị.

The only exception to this rule is the pronoun "**m.**" In the case of "m," the **"a" remains in front of the negated verb, and "m" comes after the negated verb.**

I am not eating. → Anaghị m eri nri.

Since the pronoun **m** is in this sentence, you keep the "a" in anaghị and add **m** after anaghị to get anaghị m.

To negate a verb in the future tense, you follow the same steps as you would for the present progressive. The only difference is that instead of adding the "**- ghị**" ending to **na-**, you add the "**- ghị**" ending to **ga-**.

For example:

Onyeka is not going to eat. → Onyeka agaghị eri nri.

Step 1: Conjugate **Iri nri** into the future tense. This gives you **ga-eri nri**.

Step 2: Take the hyphen way from **ga-eri nri** and add **ghị** at the end. You now have **gaghị eri nri**.

Lastly, you put an "a" in front of **gaghị eri nri**. This gives you agaghị eri nri.

The pronoun rule still applies to the future tense. If there is a pronoun at the beginning of a sentence with a negated verb in the present progressive tense, then you don't place "a" in front of **gaghị**.

For example:
She is not going to eat. → Ọ gaghị eri nri.

The pronoun in this sentence is **she**. Since gaghị falls under the A vowel group, you use the dotted o. Notice that because there is a pronoun in this sentence, there isn't an "a" in front of gaghị.

The only exception to this rule is the pronoun "**m**." In the case of "m," the **"a" remains in front of the negated verb, and "m" comes after the negated verb.**

For example:
I am not going to eat. → Agaghị m eri nri.

Since the pronoun **m** is in this sentence, you keep the "a" in agaghị and add **m** after agaghị to get agaghị m.

Negative Commands

We use negative commands when we want to tell someone not to do something.

For example:
Don't leave!
Don't eat!

To form negative commands in Igbo, you take the following steps:

Step 1: Drop the I / Ị from the infinitive form of the verb.

Step 2: Depending on the vowel harmony of the verb root, you replace the I / Ị with an **a** / **e**. If the verb root falls under the A vowel group, then you replace the dotted i with an a. If the verb root falls under the E vowel group, then you replace the undotted i with an e.

Step 3: Add **-la** to the verb root.

For example:

Don't leave! → Ahapụla!

"To leave" in Igbo is **Ịhapụ**. First, you drop the dotted I from **Ịhapụ**, which gives you **hapụ**. **Hapụ** falls under the A vowel group, so you add an "a" in front of **hapụ**. This gives you **ahapụ**. Lastly, you add the **-la** ending to **ahapụ**, which gives you Ahapụla.

Don't wait! → Echerela!

"To wait" in Igbo is **Ichere**. First, you drop the undotted I from **Ichere**, which gives you **chere**. **Chere** falls under the E vowel group, so you add an "e" in front of **chere**. This gives you **echere**. Lastly, you add the **-la** ending to **echere**, which gives you Echerela.

Chapter 6 Skills Test

1. What is the infinitive form of a verb in Igbo?

2. How does vowel harmony affect Igbo verbs in infinitive form?

3. What is the correct way to change the verb **Ịhụ** (to see) into **present simple tense**?
   a. Hụrụ
   b. Hura
   c. Hụ
   d. Leave as is

4. How would you conjugate the verb **Ichefu** (to forget) in the **present progressive tense?**

5. Why is the Igbo present progressive tense special?

6. What is the correct pronunciation of **na-ede** (writes / is writing)?

a. NAH-EH-DEH
b. NAY-DAY
c. NEH-DEH
d. NEE-DEE

7. Conjugate **ide** (to write) into the future tense.

8. You want to tell your friend Kene to wait for you. How would you command him to do so?

9. Which of these is the correct way to write **"call them!"** in Igbo?
    a. Kpọ m!
    b. Kpọ ha!
    c. Kpọ ya!
    d. Kpọ them!

10. True or false: The past tense of **Inye** (to give) is **nyera**.

11. When do we use negative verbs?

12. Translate this sentence: Adanna did not buy food yesterday. (Food = nri, yesterday = nyahụ)

13. True or false: The negation rules for the future tense and the present progressive tense are very similar.

14. Which of these is the correct way to say **"I will not go"**?
    a. Agaghị m aga.
    b. Anaghị m eri nri.
    c. A na m aga.
    d. M na-eri nri.

15. How would you change the verb **Ịbịa** (to come) into a negative command?

16. Which of these is the correct way to say, ***"she did not buy"***?
    a. Azụtaghị m
    b. Azụtaghi ya
    c. Ọ zụtaghi
    d. Ọ azụtaghi

17. Bonus: How would you say **"I will not do it"**?

18. Write down 5 Igbo infinitives. Then, change each infinitive into the present, past, and future tenses.

19. Write down the command and negation forms for the 5 verbs you selected in question 18.

QUESTIONS

Earlier in this chapter, you learned verb tenses and negations, which help greatly in having conversations. Another aspect of conversation is asking questions. To ask a question in Igbo, you do the same thing you would in English - raise your voice at the end of a sentence. Our voices tend to get higher at the end of a question, which is how we can tell the difference between a question and a statement.

For example, say these two phrases aloud:
She is going to the store.
Is she going to the store?

Notice how your voice got higher when you asked the question? Let's try an Igbo example.

She did it! → O mere ya!

This is a statement; meaning when you say it, your voice should remain constant (the same intonation throughout).

Did she do it? → O mere ya?

This is a question, meaning when you say it, your voice should get a little bit higher toward the end.

When you ask a question in the past tense in English, the most common verb used at the beginning is *did*.

For example:
Did she cry?
Did she eat?

However, in Igbo, when you ask a past tense question, the *did* is almost always implied. This means that in order to ask a question in the past tense, all you need to do is change the verb into the past tense like you would for a statement, then raise your voice at the end.

For example:

Did she eat? → O riri nri?

Did she hold it? → O jidere ya?

When you ask a question in the present, present progressive, or future tense in English, the verbs that are most commonly used at the beginning are *is* and *are*.

For example:
Is he crying?
Is she a baby?
Are you here?
Are you going to eat?

Similar to the past tense, *is* and *are* are almost always implied in Igbo. This means that if you want to ask a question in the present, present progressive, or future tense, you change the verb the same way you would for a sentence, and then raise your voice at the end.

For example:

Is she going to eat? → O ga-eri nri?

Are you Nigerian? → Ị bụ onye Nigeria?

Is he dancing? → Ọ na-agba egwu?

Chapter Seven
ADDITIONAL PRACTICE

Now that you know the fundamentals of Igbo grammar and vocabulary words, it's time to combine all of them so you can translate and form sentences. Each group of translation exercises will have the first example done, but I recommend you go back to previous chapters because doing this will help you retain everything you've learned so far. I'm so excited that you've reached this point!

Tip: Spreading this exercise out over the course of a few days will be very helpful. You'll feel less overwhelmed because you'll be mastering the material one section at a time.

Things to Check as You Go Along:
- Parts of Speech (Chapter 3)
- Vocabulary (Chapter 3)
- Pronouns, Pronouns + Vowel Harmony (Chapter 5)
- Verbs and Tenses (Chapter 6)

Present / Present Progressive Tense Sentences

1. Chinemerem eats.

    Chinemerem na-eri nri.

2. Onyeka reads.

3. Izunna is listening.

4. Adanna prays.

5. Chioma is walking.

Present / Present Progressive Tense Sentences + Pronouns

1. She dances.

   Ọ na-agba egwu.

2. He is thinking.

3. They are waiting.

4. You are listening.

5. We run.

Present / Present Progressive Tense + Pronouns + Vocabulary

1. Today, he is eating rice.

   Taa, o na-eri osikapa.

2. She is wearing gold bracelets.

3. They are chewing fruit.

4. She thinks about corn.

5. We want chairs right now.

Past Tense Sentences

1. Adaora went.

   Adaora gara.

2. Chinemerem slept.

3. Izunna cried.

4. Ifeanyi prayed.

5. Onyeka forgot.

Past Tense Sentences + Pronouns

1. She gave.

   O nyere.

2. They danced.

3. It swallowed.

4. We found out.

5. He showered.

Past Tense Sentences + Pronouns + Vocabulary

1. She washed a car yesterday.

   Ọ sara ụgbọ ala ụnyahụ.

2. He left that house.

3. They told me.

4. We walked quickly.

5. You called again.

Future Tense (Mix)

1. Ifeanyi will be a good man.

   Ifeanyi ga-abụ nwoke ọma.

2. Kelechi will speak Igbo tomorrow.

3. Chinyere will know.

4. She will come slowly.

5. They will dance immediately.

6. We will pray.

7. I will leave.

Commands

1. Learn it!

    Mụta ya!

2. Walk!

3. Follow them!

4. Don't go!

5. Don't take it!

Negations (Mix)

1. Chimezie didn't go.

    Chimezie agaghị.

2. I am not eating.

3. He does not dance.

4. Nwando doesn't sleep.

5. Don't call him!

PART THREE
Culture and Resources

Chapter 8
IGBO LEARNING RESOURCES

Learning Igbo is something that takes time and requires a lot of determination, resources, and patience. Because of this, I've decided to create a list of resources that I feel would be very helpful in your Igbo language journey. Of course, there are many more Igbo learning resources than the ones on my list, but these are my personal favorites. Enjoy!

Websites
The following websites offer online beginner lessons, animated Igbo videos, and virtual tutoring. However, some websites on this list might require payment for certain services.

- https://ezinaulo.com/
- www.learnigbonow.com
- www.igboteacher.com
- http://www.expressigbo.org/
- https://igbostudy.com

Social Media Accounts
We spend so much time on social media these days that we may as well use it to our advantage! Also, it really helps to connect with people who are just as

interested as you are in learning the Igbo language, especially because you and your Igbo speaking friends can learn from each other. These are social media accounts that I really like:

Instagram:
- @okwuid
- @learnigbonow
- @bbcnewsigbo
- @akwukwo
- @ezinaulo.igbo
- @igbolanguage
- @myigboname
- @binoandfino
- @igbopodcast
- @obynodaddymuna
- @express.igbo

Twitter:
- @IgboProverbs_
- @IgboStudy
- @Ezinaulo
- @Asusu_Igbo
- @AkwukwoLLC
-

Facebook (*Facebook Groups*)
- Igbo Language Learners Club with EziNaUlo
- Igbo Amaka Cultural Institute

Videos
You might prefer watching Igbo being spoken so that you can hear the pronunciations of certain words or absorb the information better. Here are a few YouTube channels that I recommend:

- Bino and Fino*
- Akwukwo LLC
- Ije the World Traveler*
- Igbo Village Square
- Igbo Study
- Obyno Daddy Muna TV

These are animated kids' shows that teach kids about Africa / Igbo language, but I would recommend them for any age because they use a lot of beginner Igbo vocabulary - so don't feel self-conscious about watching them!

Tip: It also helps to listen to native Igbo speakers speak Igbo because that will help you better understand how some words should sound and help you get used to differences in dialect. Also, practicing your Igbo aloud will benefit you a lot!

Apps
Igbo on our phones = Igbo on the go! Here are some Igbo apps that are very educational and easy to use:
- Igbo 101
- Beginner Igbo
- iSabi Igbo

- Mango Languages

Books

Igbo books have a special place in my heart - not only because I wrote one, but also because my dad used them to teach me Igbo when I was very young. These are a few Igbo books that I recommend, which include children's books:

- **Ọkọwaokwu Igbo Umuaka** - Yvonne C. Mbanefo
- **Igbo Grammar: Grammatical Rules in Igbo Language** - Victor Okorochukwu
- **Ije the World Traveler** - Ijeoma Emeka
- **Igbo for Learners 1** - Okechukwu C. Ihejirika

Learning Igbo doesn't have to be limited to learning only about the language! After all, in Chapter 1, you learned that "Igbo" can be used to talk about Igbo people and Igbo land as well. I really enjoy reading, and some of the books I'm recommending to you helped me become more passionate about my Igbo heritage and keeping the language alive. If you would like to learn more about Igbo culture / history or just want to read books by Igbo authors, here are a few books that I recommend:

- **Things Fall Apart** - Chinua Achebe
- **Half of a Yellow Sun** - Chimamanda Ngozi Adichie

- ***Foreign Gods*** - Okey Ndibe
- ***The Joys of Motherhood*** - Buchi Emecheta
- ***The Bride Price*** - Buchi Emecheta
- ***The Thing Around Your Neck*** - Chimamanda Ngozi Adichie
- ***Arrow of God*** - Chinua Achebe

Chapter Nine
LIST OF IGBO NAMES

Igbo is a very beautiful language, and with a beautiful language comes beautiful names. If you are looking for potential names for your child or are curious about the meanings of some Igbo names that you've heard, look no further! I've created a list of Igbo names for you to use as much as you please. Igbo names are unisex for the most part, however there are a few that are traditionally given more to girls or boys, so I'll make a separate list for those.

Unisex Igbo Names
A
Achebe - Protected by the goddess
Afamefuna - My name will not be lost / forgotten
Alisichukwu - Do not disregard God
Anuli - Joy
Akudo - Peaceful wealth
Amarachi - Grace of God
Azubuike - The past is your strength
Akuchi - Wealth from God
Arinzechukwu - Thanks be to God / Grace of God
Akachukwu - Hand of God
Azuka - The end is better than the beginning
Azuoma - Happy ending (usually given to last born child)

B
Binyelum - Live with me

C
Chetachi - Remember God
Chiamaka - God is beautiful
Chinemerem - God does it for me / God is my provider
Chinaza / Chinazaekpere - God answers prayers
Chibueze - God is king
Chibuike - God is strength
Chibuzor - God is the leader
Chidubem - May God guide me
Chidiebube - God is glorious
Chidiebere - God is merciful
Chimezie - Let God perfect it
Chinedu - God leads
Chinyere - God gave me
Chimaobi - God knows my thoughts
Chisom - God is with me
Chukwuka - God is supreme
Chukwuma - God knows best
Chukwudi - There is God / God exists
Chinonso - God is near
Chinualumogu - May God fight for me
Chizitalu - God sent
Chizaram - God answered me
Chidinma - God is good
Chiemelie - God has won
Chiagozie - God has blessed me
Chinecherem - God thinks for me

Chisimdi - God says I shall live
Chioma - Good God / Gracious God
Chimamanda - My God will not fail
Chimdalu - Thank you God
Chidera - What God has written
Chukwuemeka - God has done great things
Chinonyerem - God be with me
Chukwudumebi - God lives with me
Chinwe / Chinwendu - God is the owner (of life)
Chinaka - God decides
Chizoba - God protect us
Chijioke - God is the holder of gifts / talent
Chinenye - God gives

D
Daberechi - Lean on God
Daluchi - Thank God

E
Eberechi - God's mercy
Ebubechi - God's glory
Elechi - Looking up to God
Enyinnaya - Father's friend

G
Ginika - What could be greater than God?
Ginikanwa - What is greater than a child?

I

Ifunanya - Love
Ifeoma - Good / Beautiful thing
Ifeyinwa - Nothing compares to a child
Iheanacho - What everyone is looking for / Desire
Ikemefuna - My strength is not in vain
Ijeoma - Safe journey
Ifeanyi / Ifeanyichukwu - Nothing is beyond God / God is the most powerful
Ifedimma - Something good / Beautiful thing
Isioma - Smart / Fortunate
Izunna / Izuchukwu - God's wish
Ifesinachi - Things are from God

J

Jachike - Praise God
Jachimma - Praise God

K

Kamtochukwu - Let me praise God
Kanayochukwu - Let us keep asking God
Kasiemobi - God console me
Kamsiyochukwu / Kamsiyonna - How I asked God
Kelechi / Kelechukwu / Kenechukwu - Thank God
Kelenna - Thank the Father (God)
Kosarachi - Tell it to God
Kambili - I shall live
Kanyinulia - Let us rejoice
Kosisochukwu - As it pleases God

L
Lotanna / Lotachukwu - Remember God / Remember the Father
Lebechi - Look onto God

M
Maduka - People are greater than riches
Munachimso - God is always with me
Makuachukwu - Embrace God
Mmasinachi - Beauty comes from God
Mmachi - The beauty of God / Natural beauty
Mmesoma - God's goodness

N
Ndubuisi - Life is the most important
Ndidi - Patience
Nwachukwu - Child of God
Nzubechukwu - God's wish
Nkechi / Nkechinyerem - God's gift
Ndukwe - So long as there is life
Nwadinobi - A child in God's heart
Nkemjika - The one I have is greater
Njideka - I have the best
Ngozi - Blessing
Nonyelum - Stay with me
Nwando - Child of the shade

O
Obioma - Good heart / Kindness

Obiora - Heart of the people / Loved by the public
Obiajulu - My heart is at peace
Odera - When God writes it, it is well
Ogadinma - It will be fine
Okwuchukwu - The word of God
Onyeisi - The first, winner
Onyebuchi - No man is God
Onyekachi - Who is greater than God?
Onyinyechi - God's gift
Ozioma - Good news
Odinaka / Odinakachukwu - It is in the hands of God
Ogemdi - My time will come
Ogochukwu - God's favor
Ogechi - God's timing
Osinachi - It comes from God
Onyema / Onyemaechi - Who knows tomorrow?

S
Somadina - I will not be alone
Somtochukwu - Praise God with me
Sopuruchi - Honor God

T
Tochukwu - Praise God
Tobechukwu / Tobenna - Start praising God

U
Uchenna / Uchechi - God's plan / Will of God
Uloaku - House of wealth

Uzoma - Good way
Uzoamaka - The way is beautiful
Ugosinachi - Honor comes from God
Uzochukwu - God's way
Ugonna / Ugochukwu - Glory of God
Ugochinyere - God given gift

Y
Yadilichukwu - Leave it to God
Yobanna - Ask God

Z
Zeruwa - Beware of the world
Zikora / Zikoranachidi - Show the world (there is God)

Traditionally Female Names:
A
Adaeze - Daughter of a king, princess
Adanna / Adannaya - Father's daughter, usually given to the oldest daughter
Adaobi - First daughter in a household
Adaku - Daughter of wealth
Adaolisa - Daughter of God
Adaugo - Beautiful daughter
Adamma - Beautiful daughter
Adaora / Adaoha - Daughter of all
Agbomma - Beautiful young woman
Akunna / Akunnaya - Her father's wealth

E
Ezinne - Great mother

N
Nnenna / Nnennaya - Her father's mother
Nneoma - Good mother
Nneka - Mother is supreme
Nnedimma - Mother is good
Nwamaka - The child is beautiful
Nkiruka - The best is yet to come

O
Olanna - Father's jewel
Obiageli - Born into wealth
Obianuju - She came from plenty

U
Urenna - Father's pride
Ujunwa - Many children

Traditionally Male Names:
A
Amadi - Citizen
Amaechi - Nobody knows tomorrow / A family never closes

E
Ezenna - Father's king
Ezeudo - King of peace

I
Ikenna - God's strength

J
Jidenna - Hold on to God / father

K
Kalu - God of thunder

N
Nnamdi - My father is alive
Nwabueze - A child is king

O
Obinna - Father's heart, the heart of God

Chapter Ten
SKILLS TEST ANSWERS

Chapter 2 Unit 1
1. C
2. A
3. B
4. C
5. Ụdaume
6. 28 consonants, 9 double consonants
7. A and D
8. Answers may vary.

Chapter 2 Unit 2
1. B
2. A group, E group
3. A
4. Light vowel group
5. Heavy vowel group
6. C

Skills Test - Igbo Numbers
1. Iri atọ na asaa
2. Iri (10) + number less than 10 + "na" (and) + another number less than 10
3. Otu nari na iri isii na asatọ
4. False

5. Nke iri na asaa
6. Nke iri asaa na ise
7. 56 - Iri ise na isii
   37 - Iri atọ na asaa
   148 - Otu nari na iri anọ na asatọ
   79 - Iri asaa na itoolu
   93 - Iri itoolu na atọ
   831 - Nari asatọ na iri atọ na otu
   1,477 - Otu puku na nari anọ na iri asaa na asaa
   3,232 - Puku atọ na nari abụọ na iri atọ na abụọ

Chapter 4 (Tone Marks)

1. Akwa (egg) = Àkwá, Akwa (cry) = Ákwá, Akwa (cloth) = Ákwà
2. Egwu (dance / play / music) = Égwú, Egwu (fear) = Égwù

Chapter 5

1. Wording may vary, but main point is: The vowel harmony of a verb in a sentence determines whether the dotted or undotted I / O is used. If the verb belongs in the A group, you use the dotted I / O. If the verb belongs in the E group, you use the undotted I / O.
2. Third person pronouns are used when someone or something / a group of people or things are being talked about. In the Igbo

language, they are: ha (they), o / ọ (he, she, it), and ya (he, she, it).
3. A, B
4. First person, second person, third person, possessive, demonstrative, and interrogative
5. D
6. Ha means "they / theirs," while ya means "she / he / it / hers / his / its / her / him"
7. A
8. A
9. Answers may vary.

Cumulative Test: Chapters 1 - 5

1. 2, A group + E group
2. Gị, Ị
3. 36
4. Abịdịị
5. A
6. A E I Ị O Ọ U Ụ
7. C
8. A, E
9. *A group* vowels (A, Ị, Ọ, Ụ) are always paired with each other in Igbo words, while E group vowels (E, I, O, U) are paired with one another.
10. 7
11. Niger - Congo, Key characteristic: They are tonal, meaning that they use pitch to

    distinguish between words with the same spelling
12. D
13. 3
14. False
15. False
16. C
17. A
18. Southeastern Nigeria
19. 86 - Iri asatọ na isii
    43 - Iri anọ na atọ
    194 - Otu nari na iri itoolu na anọ
    221 - Nari abụọ na iri abụọ na otu
    546 - Nari ise na iri anọ na isii
    1,341 - Otu puku na nari atọ na iri anọ na otu
    3,987 - Puku atọ na nari itoolu na iri asatọ na asaa
20. Ụdaelu, Ụdaala, Ụdansuda
21. True
22. False
23. Answers may vary.

Chapter 6

1. i / ị + the root of the verb
2. If the verb root falls under the A vowel group, then the "I" in front is dotted. If the verb root falls under the E vowel group, then the "I" in front is undotted.
3. A

4. Na-echefu
5. A majority of Igbo verbs use the same conjugation for both the present simple tense and the present progressive tense.
6. C
7. Ga-ede
8. Chere m! (Wait for me!)
9. B
10. False
11. We use negative verbs when we are talking about an action that does not happen, did not happen, or will not happen.
12. Adanna azụtaghị nri ụnyahụ.
13. True
14. A
15. Abịala!
16. C
17. A gaghị m eme ya.
18. Answers may vary. (follow rules in Chapter 6)
19. Answers may vary. (follow rules in Chapter 6)

Chapter 7

Present / Present Progressive Tense Sentences
1. Chinemerem na-eri nri.
2. Onyeka na-agụ.
3. Izunna na-ege ntị.
4. Adanna na-ekpe ekpere.
5. Chioma na-aga ije.

Present / Present Progressive + Pronouns
1. Ọ na-agba egwu.
2. O na eche echiche.
3. Ha na-echere.
4. I na-ege ntị.
5. Anyị na-agba ọsọ.

Present / Present Progressive + Pronouns + Vocabulary
1. Taa, o na-eri osikapa.
2. O na-eyiri mgba aka ọla edo.
3. Ha na-ata mkpuru osisi.
4. O na-eche echiche gbasara ọka.
5. Anyị chọrọ oche ugbu a.

Past Tense
1. Adaora gara.
2. Chinemerem rahụrụ ura.
3. Izunna bere akwa.
4. Ifeanyi kpere ekpere.
5. Onyeka chefuru.

Past Tense + Pronouns
1. O nyere.
2. Ha gbara egwu.
3. O loro.
4. Anyị chọpụtara.
5. Ọ sara ahụ.

Past Tense + Pronouns + Vocabulary
1. Ọ sara ụgbọ ala ụnyahụ.

2. Ọ hapụrụ ụlọ ahụ.
3. Ha gwara m.
4. Anyị gara ije ọsịsọ
5. Ị kpọrọ ọzọ.

Future Tense (Mix)
1. Ifeanyi ga-abụ nwoke ọma.
2. Kelechi ga-asụ Igbo echi.
3. Chinyere ga-ama.
4. Ọ ga-abịa nwayọ nwayọ.
5. Ha ga-agba egwu ozugbo.
6. Anyị ga-ekpe ekpere.
7. A ga m ahapụ. / M ga ahapụ.

Commands
1. Mụta ya!
2. Ga ije!
3. Soro ha!
4. Agala!
5. Ewerela ya!

Negations (Mix)
1. Chimezie agaghị.
2. Agaghị m eri nri.
3. Ọ naghị agba egwu.
4. Nwando anaghị arahụ ura.
5. Akpọla ya!

Acknowledgements

I never imagined myself writing a book at seventeen, and I couldn't have done it without my support system.

I have to start off by thanking my parents, Dr. Onyebuchi Nwanze and Mrs. Chinyere Nwanze, for teaching me the Igbo language and instilling in me a deep passion for my culture. You inspire me to work as hard as I can in anything I do, and I'm eternally grateful that I get to call you my parents. I don't know where I would be without your love and encouragement.

I would also like to thank my little sister, Onyeka Nwanze, for drawing the pictures seen in Chapter 3. Thank you so much for being willing to help me with the artistic aspect of my book. I love you, sis!

To my community at St. Eugene's Igbo Catholic Church, which has stood by me since I started lecturing in Igbo at the age of ten, thank you all for the motivational messages you have showered me with over the years. To my Auntie Helen Egbuniwe, thank you for believing in me and for giving me the reading that led to my love of professing the Word of God in my native language.

To Nia Sade Akinyemi, thank you for giving me the opportunity to be an intern for your brand, *The Literary*

Revolutionary, and helping me throughout the publishing process.

A very special thanks to the Igbo Catholic Young Adult Organization, whose mission to educate the youth on Igbo culture served as one of my inspirations for this book. We truly are the future.

Finally, I would like to thank God for helping me through the stressful times and ultimately blessing me with this rewarding experience.

Made in the USA
Las Vegas, NV
08 April 2022